Consciousness and the Unconscious

DAVID ARCHARD

Senior Lecturer in Philosophy, Ulster Polytechnic

OPEN COURT PUBLISHING COMPANY

LA SALLE, ILLINOIS 61301

OPEN COURT and the above logo are registered in the
U.S. patent and trademark office.

OC850   10 9 8 7 6 5 4 3 2 1

ISBN: 0-87548-435-2

Published by arrangement with Hutchinson Publishing Group Ltd.

First published 1984

Photoset in 11 on 12 pt Baskerville by
Kelly Typesetting Limited
Bradford-on-Avon, Wiltshire

Printed and bound in Great Britain by
Anchor Brendon Ltd,
Tiptree, Essex

Library of Congress Cataloging in Publication Data

Archard, David.
Consciousness and the unconscious.

(Problems of modern European thought)
Includes bibliographies and index
1. Subconsciousness—history.   2. Freud, Sigmund, 1856–1939.
3. Lacan, Jacques, 1901– .   4. Psychoanalysis and Philosophy—
History.   5. Psychoanalysis—France—history.   I. Title.   II.
Series.
BF315.A67   1984   154   84–1011

ISBN 0-87548-435-2

*Consciousness
and the
Unconscious*

PROBLEMS OF
MODERN EUROPEAN THOUGHT

Contents

Editors' foreword

During most of the twentieth century, philosophers in the English-speaking world have had only partial and fleeting glimpses of the work of their counterparts in continental Europe. In the main, English-language philosophy has been dominated by the exacting ideals of conceptual analysis and even of formal logic, while 'continental philosophy' has ventured into extensive substantive discussions of literary, historical, psycho-analytic and political themes. With relatively few exceptions, the relations between the two traditions have been largely uncomprehending and hostile.

In recent years, however, continental writers such as Heidegger, Adorno, Sartre, de Beauvoir, Habermas, Foucault, Althusser, Lacan, and Derrida have been widely read in English translation, setting the terms of theoretical debate in such fields as literature, social theory, cultural studies, marxism, and feminism. The suspicions of the analytical philosophers have not, however, been pacified; and the import of such continental philosophy has mostly been isolated from original philosophical work in English.

PROBLEMS OF MODERN EUROPEAN THOUGHT series is intended to help break down this isolation. The books in the series will be original philosophical essays in their own right, from authors familiar with the procedures of analytical philosophy. Each book will present a well-defined range of themes from continental philosophy, and will presuppose little, if any formal philosophical training of its readers.

Alan Montefiore
Jonathan Rée

Acknowledgements

For several years I have been fortunate to know Stephen Mills as a friend and as a fellow philosopher. My views on the general nature of philosophy and concerning specific philosophical topics have been immeasurably influenced by that friendship. This book is no exception and I thank him for the time and care he took in discussing its contents. Chapters 1 and 2, in particular, owe much to his critical suggestions.

My series editors at Hutchinson, Jonathan Rée and Alan Montefiore, have both shown immense patience, thoughtfulness and skill in their treatment of the many drafts submitted them. Countless infelicities of style and inadequacies in argument have been eliminated due to their care. Claire L'Enfant at Hutchinson has, through her kindness and efficiency, made the normally fraught relation between author and publisher a pleasure. Various people have read earlier drafts of all or parts of this book. I would like to thank them for their criticisms and suggestions, in particular, Kim Davies, Pete Dews, Jean-Jacques Lecercle and Michael Slote.

None of the above should, of course, be held responsible for the final outcome of their advice.

I would like to thank Tony Morris for his constant encouragement and support of my work; thanks are due also to John and Colin for their efforts in uncovering material for Chapter 5.

Last, but by no means least, love and gratitude to those friends who made my life tolerable during the writing of this book, especially Margaret, Valerie, Keith, and Jacqueline.

The book is dedicated to B. and H. H.

David Archard
Belfast

Introduction

This book is about the concept of 'the unconscious' as it has been defined, defended and criticized in recent Continental writing. It necessarily concentrates on the ideas of Sigmund Freud. For most, if not all, contemporary writers 'the unconscious' is merely an agreed, abbreviated, rendering of '(Freud's concept of) the unconscious'. This is a readily understandable but unfortunate assumption. For, in different ways and contexts, it leads to both an understatement and an overstatement of Freud's importance. There is understatement when it is implied or stated that *all* of Freud's work can be summarized by the term, and there is overstatement when it is implied or stated that Freud invented the term or, at any rate, is the only writer to have given it any meaning.

Such overstatement is compounded when Freud is taken at his own (immodest) word and described as having successfully inaugurated a Copernican revolution in thinking about the human being. 'As Freud has clearly shown', or 'psychoanalysis demonstrates', or phrases of this nature, introduce arguments which employ the concept of 'the unconscious' as if it were the undisputed finding of an agreed and well-established science. Moreover, the significance frequently accorded to this 'discovery' is not inconsiderable. 'The unconscious', it is said, is a 'fact' whose correct understanding entails the demise of an entire tradition of philosophical thought about the human subject, language and social relations. To refuse to accept the concept of 'the unconscious' is thus both to ignore the evidence of an accredited science and to cling obstinately to an archaic philosophical conception of human beings.

The trouble with all of this is the failure to distinguish a number of distinct questions: In what precise sense, if any, is Freud's concept of 'the unconscious' peculiar to him? Which concepts of 'the unconscious' are incompatible with which philosophies of mind or of the subject?

9

How much is entailed by acceptance of a Freudian concept of 'the unconscious'? Are we bound also to accept his ideas, for instance, concerning the sexual instincts and their somatic basis, the mechanisms of the psychic apparatus and his theory of language? In other words, what, concerning 'the unconscious', has Freud so 'clearly shown', and in what, if any, sense is this intelligible and perhaps also true?

A proper answer to the last question is important for the following reason. In those theoretical disciplines within the English-speaking world where, over recent years, the influence of pychoanalysis has been most marked – namely feminism, cultural and literary criticism, certain forms of Marxism – it is French readings of Freud that have been particularly influential. In this context, it is not simply the idea of an 'unconscious' that we are enjoined to accept as true, but a specifically Freudian understanding of this concept and a specifically French understanding of Freud. The greatest danger attached to any cultural importation of intellectual systems is that it invites unqualified acceptance or rejection of the whole. What is possibly of some value is simply offered at an unacceptably high intellectual price. While it would do Freud a great disservice to suggest that his sole achievement lay in licensing an intelligible (and perhaps, perforce, relatively trivial) use of the term 'unconscious', he would also be ill-served by a presentation of his entire thought in a form which requires immediate return rather than sale. It is therefore crucial to understand which Freud and which concept of 'the unconscious' are on offer.

This Introduction seeks to provide some context for the discussions of these questions that follow. The concept of 'the unconscious' has been used in philosophy, but, in its Freudian sense at least, the concept was formulated, defended, amplified and modified in the context of the medical and therapeutic project of 'psychoanalysis'. The nature of psychoanalysis, philosophy and their relationship does not permit easy exchange of ideas – especially when extravagant claims are made for the significance of such an exchange. This is not to deny the possible value of some mutual encroachment, only to state the need for a clarification of its proper limits.

The emergence of psychoanalytic theory was an especially complicated process, and one inseparable from the career and personality of its creator. In no other instance has the itinerary of a thought been so markedly that of its thinker. In its earliest formulations and most decisive moments psychoanalysis simply was Freud's self-analysis.

(And what, for some, is the mark of ruthless and painfully honest self-investigation shows, for others, the personalized character of a mere pseudo-science.)

However, during Freud's lifetime psychoanalysis was not merely a body of theory. It acquired and developed an international organization whose members owed personal loyalty – if not devotion – to Freud as a condition of affiliation. The likening of the psychoanalytic movement to a church was much favoured – and not only by critics of Freud. If the comparison is apt then, indisputably, Freud reigned alone as its supreme pontiff. Like a church, the movement had its heretics who were publicly reviled and excommunicated for their departure from canonical truth – Alfred Adler, Wilhelm Stekel, Carl Jung and Otto Rank. Arguably those who remained within the official movement, and loyal to Freud, were able to do so by combining, in different degrees, personal sycophancy and intellectual unoriginality. It should be added that continued membership of the movement meant a great deal. At stake were the terms and conditions of psychoanalytic practice and, consequently, the very right to earn a living as an analyst. And, from its beginnings, psychoanalysis has prospered as a large and lucrative profession.

The history of the psychoanalytic movement was one not only of bitter personal conflict and division, but also of individual tragedy – the number of broken relationships and broken lives is astonishing, and alarming, by any standards. To what extent Freud can personally be held responsible for this human cost is debatable and, for our purposes, beside the point. The fact remains that, within the movement, Freud established a certain tenor of intellectual debate which made dispassionate criticism of his work difficult and outright heterodoxy painful and hazardous. To disagree publicly with Freud beyond a certain point was to attack the very foundations of the psychoanalytic movement, and moreover, as many openly stated, to rebel against one's father figure.

Many writers on the psychoanalytic movement have drawn attention to the tensions which resulted from the contradictory impulses promoting its development – between the pursuit of objective scientific truth and the successful institution of a distinct profession with its own standards of internal conduct and management, between the creation of an intellectual community of peers and the fostering of a cult of the movement's founding personality. It would, of course, be wrong to imply that all theoretical disciplines other than psychoanalysis are exempt from such pressures. Equally it would be absurd to dismiss Freudianism out of hand as no more than a tyrant's lie, repeated by cowed subjects. Nevertheless, in assessing Freud's characterization and defence of his theory, it is always worth remembering to what extent psychoanalysis represents a very special case of institutionalized theory.

Here it is interesting – and instructive – to note the parallels between Freud and Jacques Lacan. Lacan is the single most important source of French Freudianism, and his ideas will be treated extensively in Chapter 3. Like Freud's, Lacan's career was marked by institutional struggles, bitter personal disagreements and, in its latter stages, a role as father figure. The French psychoanalytic movement dates back to the 1920s, but in 1945 the Paris Psychoanalytic Society, to which Lacan had belonged since 1934, had only eleven members. A vigorous recruiting campaign increased its numbers but, in the 1950s, tensions appeared. These arose over the theoretical status of psychoanalysis and proposals to create a psychoanalytic training institute. Then, and subsequently, Lacan passionately opposed the construction of psychoanalysis as an essentially medical, neurobiological discipline and its administration within an overly rigid and authoritarian structure. At the same time, Lacan himself was subject to severe criticism over the unorthodox nature of his personal psychoanalytic practice – in particular, his preference for extremely short analytic sessions. In 1953, after a vote of no confidence, Lacan resigned from the presidency of the Paris Society and, with others, helped to form the French Psychoanalytic Society. The latter was subsequently excluded from the official movement, the International Psychoanalytic Association. It is this context which explains why Lacan's celebrated 'Rome address' ('The Function and Field of Speech and Language in Psychoanalysis'), delivered in 1953, was not simply a theoretical defence of psychoanalysis as a human science, irreducible to neurophysiology, but an open and vehement attack upon all authoritarian forms of organization in the psychoanalytic movement.

The price asked of the French Psychoanalytic Society for readmission into the International Association was the exclusion of Lacan. In 1963 the French Psychoanalytic Society duly removed Lacan's name from its list of training analysts and, as a result, split. The anti-Lacan group, The French Psychoanalytic Association, secured entry into the

International Association in 1965. Lacan formed his own group, the École Freudienne de Paris, in 1964 and, in the same year, he moved his teaching seminar from Saint Anne Hospital to the École Normale Supérieure. The two events provided Lacan with a public platform for the promulgation and promotion of his distinctive theory. Lacan's mission in the School was to reconstruct psychoanalysis as a 'cultural theory' which remained supremely faithful to the Freudian text. The latter had to be understood in those specifically Lacanian ways which, as will be seen later, owe much to the disciplines of linguistics and anthropology. Thus Freudianism was separated from the physiological and biological sciences and offered to the human sciences. At the same time, Lacan's Paris seminars exerted, throughout the 1960s and 1970s, a major influence on those French intellectual 'stars' who regularly attended them – in a way which curiously parallels the role of Alexandre Kojève's lectures on Hegel in the 1930s.

The irony of Lacan's attempt to break away from the rigid and authoritarian institutionalism of the official psychoanalytic movement was that he created the conditions for another church – a 'Lacanian' sect whose members were bound to the canonical texts and undisputed personal leadership of Lacan himself. One small, but telling, example: the official journal of the Freudian School, *Scilicet*, published all articles anonymously save those of Lacan himself. Some found the atmosphere intolerable and left in 1969 to form the 'Fourth Group'.

The end came in an appropriately Lacanian fashion. In 1980 Lacan announced that the School had a problem and that the solution lay in its dissolution. Inevitably, subsequent debate over the decision centred on whether the School, as Lacan's creation, served only to teach his work and thus could rightfully be dissolved by him personally, or whether this act finally demonstrated Lacan's consistent, but wholly intolerable, authoritarian and paternalistic control of the 'School'. That Freudian psychoanalysis enjoys its high status in France is due in large measure to the influence of Lacan; that this should have been achieved at the expense of so much personal bitterness, so many scissions and, ultimately, so much dependence on the work and personality of a single figure is ironic tribute to Lacan's fidelity to Freud.

Of course, the personal shortcomings of theorists are no argument against their theories – though such failings are, for obvious reasons, more unacceptable in a psychoanalyst than someone from another discipline. Moreover, both Freud and Lacan undoubtedly established

13

individual 'styles' for the presentation and defence of their respective work which are at variance with the ideals of rational, intellectual discussion. Perhaps the *hauteur* (to be charitable) of its major thinkers is a function of the enforced, defensive insularity of psychoanalysis, its felt need to establish and sustain itself apart from other disciplines. Certainly, both Freud and Lacan were jealous for the specific achievements of psychoanalysis. They viewed with extreme suspicion, if not outright hostility, intellectual work outside psychoanalysis which was seen to ignore, bowdlerize or travesty these achievements.

This is especially true of philosophy – a term which Lacan and Freud were inclined to employ in a pejorative way. In later years Freud felt able to acknowledge the extent to which, for instance, Nietzsche and Schopenhauer intuited philosophically what psychoanalysis subsequently established scientifically. In his earlier work, and particularly with respect to 'the unconscious', Freud viewed psychoanalysis as revealing what philosophy was congenitally incapable of accepting. Freud is not the first thinker to have rewritten the history of ideas with a view to self-aggrandisement, but it is worth setting the record straight.

Lancelot Whyte's curious, and now somewhat neglected, book, *The Unconscious before Freud*, tries to establish an intellectual history of 'the unconscious', which, without detracting from Freud's originality, places his work in its proper context. Whyte collates views, presented in direct quotation or summary, from a vast array of Western thinkers which all demonstrate an assurance that unconscious mental processes of some sort do, and indeed must, exist. Furthermore, Whyte argues that the notion of 'the unconscious' had become a commonplace of European thought in the decade *before* that of Freud's first published writings. Following the enormous success of Eduard von Hartmann's *Philosophy of the Unconscious* (1868), at least six books were published during the 1870s with the word 'unconscious' in their titles. That Freud should largely have ignored such previous work and vastly exaggerated his originality in using the term 'unconscious' is characteristic of him. It is curious, however, that Freud should have thought the idea of an 'unconscious' to be the main obstacle to public acceptance of his theories. At the end of the nineteenth century a number of different theories of 'the unconscious' were widespread and widely discussed. Almost certainly, Whyte suggests, it was less Freud's use of the term 'unconscious' than his definition of it in exclusively sexual terms which provoked hostility. Certainly, in making the concept of 'the

14

unconscious' his own, Freud made his own concept of 'the unconscious' the distinctive feature of the new psychoanalytic science.

The result, in part, has been to set psychoanalysis and philosophy in false opposition over the question of 'the unconscious'. The simple fact is that there are senses and uses of the term 'unconscious' which philosophy – to employ the term generically and loosely – does not find troubling. In objecting to Freud's concept of 'the unconscious' philosophers are not rejecting the whole idea of there being unconscious mental processes. 'Of course there are, indeed there must be unconscious mental processes', or some such statement, is all too often naïvely presented as a self-evident proposition which establishes both the credentials of psychoanalysis – which only points out this obvious fact – and the inherent fallibility of philosophy – which is presumed to deny it.

One reason for this naïve view is the false belief that philosophy as a whole subscribes to the 'Cartesian' identification of the mental and consciousness, that is the assertion that all mental events or states are ones of which the individual is immediately and certainly conscious or aware. 'Cartesian' was introduced within quotation marks as an indication that this doctrine oversimplifies the actual work of Descartes. Nevertheless, it is conventional to understand the Cartesian philosophy of mind as committed to such an identification. And, clearly, on such an account Freud's concept of 'the unconscious', indeed any notion of unconscious mental events, must be rejected as incoherent. Cartesianism, however, is understood by philosophers to consist of more than this single doctrine. Consequently, the concern of many writers to depict Freud as an anti-Cartesian philosopher of mind misreads his philosophical significance, and leaves it open to nominally 'anti-Cartesian' thinkers to interpret Freud in a quite Cartesian way.

Descartes is accredited with the identification of the mental and consciousness. But he is also celebrated for having subscribed to dualism – the belief that the individual human being consists of both a mind and a body, interrelated but essentially distinct in kind, the former being irreducibly mental and the latter irreducibly physical. Further, Descartes held the rationalist conviction that the individual can, totally and sufficiently, know and express all that is, in principle, knowable about himself/herself and the external world. In depicting the human mind as a self-aware consciousness able rationally and fully to comprehend itself, Cartesian philosophy seems, fairly obviously, wrong. Nevertheless, it would be an error to conclude that the respects in which, and reasons why, it is wrong are precisely those respects in which, and reasons why, Freudianism is right. Freud and Descartes were not the respective authors of mutually exclusive or jointly exhaustive philosophies of mind.

It is, after all, perfectly consistent with some features of Cartesianism to maintain that unconscious mental processes do exist, but that these are not reducible to physical processes; or that the individual is incapable of fully and rationally comprehending himself/herself, but that this self must nevertheless be understood dualistically; or, again, that 'the unconscious', if it exists, has exactly those characteristics of the conscious mind, namely ideas, desires, beliefs, etc., excepting the fact that these latter are, in the case of 'the unconscious', ones of which the individual is unaware.

To interpret the dispute between philosophy and psychoanalysis over the question of 'the unconscious' as Freudianism versus Cartesianism is, thus, doubly mistaken. In the first place, there are those who refuse the Cartesian identification of conscious and mental, yet subscribe to a notion of 'unconscious' which is not specifically Freudian. Second, there are others who accept Freud's concept of 'the unconscious', but understood in terms which remain, in some important senses, Cartesian. Lancelot Whyte maintains that it was Descartes who stimulated thinkers to explore the possible existence of unconscious mentality and thus prepared the ground for Freud's own work. But, whether or not Freud is, in this sense, a post-Cartesian, it is a misleading simplification to view him as simply and straightforwardly an anti-Cartesian.

The philosophical significance of the Freudian notion of 'the unconscious' is thus more complex than some of its protagonists would polemically claim. In part, as this Introduction has tried to indicate, this is because a concept, developed in a unique psychoanalytic context, has been imported into a particular philosophical context. What 'Freud has so clearly shown' is neither unambiguous nor indisputably true. By means of a study of Continental writing on the subject of 'the unconscious', the rest of this book will attempt to show why.

Further reading

On the history of the psychoanalytic movement, Paul Roazen's monumental *Freud and His Followers* (London 1979) is an invaluable guide. Freud's own role is fairly and astutely depicted, and the precise differences Freud had with others are concisely outlined. Another book by Roazen, *Brother Animal: The Story of Freud and Tausk* (London 1970) documents a forgotten episode, and provides a most revealing and carefully judged picture of Freud's personal character.

On the history of the French psychoanalytic movement, and Lacan's dramatic role within it, Sherry Turkle's *Psychoanalytic Politics: Freud's French Revolution* (London 1982) is invaluable, and its somewhat journalistic style of reportage makes for a much racier account.

Lancelot Whyte's *The Unconscious before Freud*, first published in 1960, has been reissued with an introduction by Arthur Koestler (London 1979).

For a marvellous introduction to the 'flavour' of psychoanalysis, which also provides a useful summary of the main doctrines of Freud, see Janet Malcolm's *Psychoanalysis: The Impossible Profession* (London 1982).

1

The unconscious

It is unfortunate – for reasons given in the Introduction – that the term 'the unconscious' should have been taken as an abbreviation of 'Freud's concept of the unconscious'. Equally, it would be unfortunate if 'Freud's theory' were read elliptically as 'Freud's theory (of the unconscious)'. And for two reasons. First, there is clearly much more to Freudianism than the postulation of unconscious mental processes. Indeed, the Freudian notion of the unconscious is itself set within a complex and comprehensive account of human personality. In very crude and simple terms, Freudianism, taken as a whole, is a theory of how and why human beings, born with certain pre-given biological features, acquire their personal characteristics. Thus Freud offers a theory of personal development, of gender and sexuality, and of the relationship between the biological or natural and the social or cultural.

But Freudianism is also, as the Introduction stressed, related to psychoanalytic practice. It would be naïve to ignore the therapeutic context to Freud's notion of 'the unconscious'. After all, the psychoanalytic cure involves a making conscious of what previously had been unconscious; and this disclosure has language as a key instrument. Of course, Freud's views about the limits and character of this 'talking cure' – as it was aptly and famously entitled by an early patient – underwent considerable change. But, significantly, his estimation of the therapeutic possibilities of psychoanalysis both enriched and was informed by his understanding of 'the unconscious'.

The second reason for caution when speaking of 'Freud's theory of the unconscious' is that Freud's views on the nature of unconscious mental processes changed significantly throughout his life. Indeed this chapter will show how Freud came to realize that the disjunction 'conscious'/'unconscious' was unfortunate in so far as it focused

18

attention on distinctions other than those he believed most important to psychoanalytic investigation.

It is conventional to divide Freud's work into an early and late period. The former includes the classic studies of dreams (1900–1), the psychopathology of everyday life (1901), and jokes (1905), and the three essays on sexuality (1905). Freud did not in fact make any systematic statement about the nature of unconscious mental processes until after 1910, and his classic theoretical paper on 'the unconscious' was written in 1915. The principal works of Freud's 'late' period are *Beyond the Pleasure Principle* (1920), *The Ego and the Id* (1923), and *Inhibitions, Symptoms and Anxiety* (1926). These later studies stated and developed the concepts of Id, Ego and Superego which, in broad terms, displaced those of unconscious and conscious.

The foregoing comments are intended to set Freud's notion of 'the unconscious' in its proper context. They should not be taken as denying the central importance of this notion to Freud's work as a whole. Significantly, most of Freud's popular introductions to psychoanalysis begin with a defence of such a concept. Freud feels obliged to show the legitimacy of even using the term 'unconscious', and thus seeks to expose the intellectual 'prejudice' of equating the psychic with what is conscious.

To this end he appeals to the easily intuitable and unexceptionable fact that consciousness is 'discontinuous', that it is experienced as incomplete and containing gaps. Freud's simplest example is this. I am now thinking a particular idea. Momentarily distracted my concentration turns to the thought of something else and during this time I am not aware of the idea which previously occupied me. The source of distraction removed, I return to thinking the original idea. The same idea is, while I am distracted by something else, 'missing' from consciousness but presumed intact between its first and second appearances. To answer such a case Freud proposes that the idea in question be regarded as 'unconscious' in the intervening period.

In speaking of 'discontinuity', Freud, of course, conflates 'consciousness of X' (where 'X' is an idea, thought or whatever) with 'consciousness as a whole'. On Freud's use of the example, all ideas of which we are ever conscious will be 'unconscious' most of the time. Indeed, at any one time, all but a very few ideas will be 'unconscious'. Moreover, it is worth noting that 'unconscious' is used here, as it is generally in English, as a predicate of the object, the idea, rather than of the subject.

However, Freud takes his argument to license a move from the relatively unobjectionable proposition – all the ideas we are ever aware of will also, at other times, be ones of which we are unaware – to the more contentious view that there are unconscious mental processes to which ideas, while and to the extent that we are unaware of them, belong. This is principally because Freud believed that psychology must be explanatory and not merely descriptive. He takes the proper object of psychology to be the psychic or mental as such. Questions of the relation of mental processes to physiological ones are suspended. Introducing a notion of unconscious mental processes secures a continuum of the psychic which can then be the object of meaningful psychological explanation.

According to Freud, those who continue to equate the psychic with what is conscious either cannot explain the 'gaps' in experience, or are compelled to explain them in terms of the nonpsychical, that is as physical or physiological processes. Such a psychology, Freud supposed, either cannot offer an adequate explanation of the mental or has to merge into physiology. This is an overstated disjunction, however: one could speak of capacities for consciousness, or of an idea being such that it could be recalled to awareness, and thus avoid supposing the existence of unconscious psychic processes.

Nevertheless, given Freud's use of the disjunction, some account has to be offered of what distinguishes a conscious process from any other. His own account is not a good one. We are not, for Freud, conscious *of* psychic processes. *In itself* the psychic is unknowable. Rather some psychic processes have consciousness as an attribute or 'quality' which can directly be 'perceived'. The notion of consciousness as a perceived property is odd, if only because that which I 'perceive' must necessarily be that of which I am conscious. Even so, it is important to make clear the sense in which Freud intends the phrase 'unconscious psychic process'. Any psychic process is unconscious in the sense that it cannot be the perceived, or directly known, object of consciousness. A properly unconscious psychic process is unconscious in the further and more specific sense that it does not have the perceived attribute of consciousness.

Those psychic processes which are conscious can be described under their different experiential aspects – as thoughts, fears, wishes, remembrances, etc. Since the psychic is considered by Freud to be continuous, comprising both conscious and unconscious, he thinks it legitimate to

20

extend such descriptions to unconscious psychic processes. We can thus talk of unconscious memories, wishes, ideas, etc. This is to be understood as meaning that such and such a psychic event, though unconscious, would appear in the form of a wish, memory or whatever, were it to have the additional attribute of consciousness. Psychology acquires a proper scientific status by taking as its object the continuum of psychic processes described in the terms of their actual or conditionalized conscious appearances.

However well such arguments found the special claim of psychology, they only license a particular, and comparatively limited, usage of the term 'unconscious', one that Freud himself dubs *descriptive*. Used in this way, 'unconscious' merely means the absence from a psychical process of the attribute of consciousness. The claims of psychoanalysis require the difference between conscious and unconscious to be something more. In particular, unconscious mental processes have a role to play in determining the character of conscious mental processes. Freud adopts the example of post-hypnotic suggestion to illustrate such a possibility.

Under hypnosis an individual is ordered to carry out a certain action at a certain moment after being awakened from his or her hypnotic state. On awakening the individual may have no memory of having been hypnotized. Yet, at the pre-arranged moment, s/he performs the requisite action and does it consciously. Freud sees no alternative but to describe the order as 'latent' or 'unconscious' during the post-hypnotic period. Now this example differs significantly from that of distraction given previously. The order is not merely absent or latent; it is both unconscious and *active*. That is, the conscious execution of the ordered action may be said to eventuate as a result of the unconscious order.

Freud used such examples to familiarize his audience with the kind of evidence to be gained from the observation of pathological individuals. The phrase 'unconscious and active' also serves to designate those ideas that may be found in the minds of hysterical patients. It is principally with such pathological evidence that Freud introduced what he called the *dynamic* conception of the unconscious. In most of his expository accounts, Freud's move from a descriptive to a dynamic use of the term 'unconscious' is closely related to a distinction between the conscious and the preconscious. The latter is the quality of those ideas which are merely latent and which the individual is able to recall without difficulty. The term 'unconscious' proper now designates those ideas which show evidence of having been excluded from, and thus remaining inadmissible and inaccessible to, consciousness.

In so far as the distinction between conscious and unconscious is descriptive the important line of division lies between conscious on the one hand, and preconscious/unconscious on the other; whereas, for the dynamic and other senses of unconscious, the line is between unconscious and preconscious/conscious. Without being so named, it was the evidence of preconscious ideas that served the introductory argument for the use of the term 'unconscious'. Arguably then, the earlier examples are relatively unimportant. What matters is not that an idea should be unconscious, but that it should be a certain kind of unconscious idea, namely one that has causal efficacy in relation to conscious ideas. Moreover, as will shortly be seen, even preconscious ideas can possess this causal efficacy, so that Freud is really talking about certain kinds of unconscious ideas having certain kinds of causal effects on conscious ideas because of their relation to consciousness.

The proper object of psychoanalysis may be defined as 'the unconscious' in the dynamic sense, and explicitly distinguished from both consciousness and preconsciousness. Freud believed that pathological evidence necessitated the use of 'unconscious' in this sense. For pedagogic purposes, however, Freud used the evidence of 'normal' phenomena to demonstrate its existence. Dreams and parapraxes – slips of the tongue, forgetfulness and errors – make the psychoanalytic theory of unconscious processes accessible to a public unfamiliar with the purely pathological material. One of his favourite examples was slips of the tongue.

An individual utters something which s/he had not intended. The phrase or word in question may or may not be meaningful in itself. In very many cases the individual may quickly realize how the slip had occurred. S/he wished, by way of a simple example, to say 'I'm going home'. Instead s/he utters the phrase, 'I'm sowing Hume'. The occurrence of this apparently meaningless sentence acquires psychological sense when s/he realizes that by going home s/he would be seeing Hugh. The intended speech and unuttered thought combined to result in the senseless phrase. In other instances the individual may not immediately recognize the reason for his or her slip. But s/he will belatedly acknowledge an explanation in terms of an unuttered thought if an intelligent listener suggests it.

In a third set of cases, the utterer of the slip can see no reason for his or her error. Moreover, s/he denies having the unexpressed thought which a listener interpolates to make sense, as in the other cases, of his or her unintended error. Freud sees no reason why one should not regard all three sets of examples as occupying a continuum. In all of them the slip of the tongue results from the interference of two intended speeches, the slip itself being a compromise between them. The last set of examples differs only in that the unexpressed and unintended speech or thought is not, and cannot be, acknowledged by the speaker. Freud suggests that such a thought is unconscious in the psychoanalytic and dynamic sense. Inaccessible to and excluded from consciousness, it nevertheless determines the character of the conscious phenomenon – the utterance – by interfering with, and thereby distorting, the intended speech of which the individual is immediately aware. By postulating and inferring such unconscious thoughts we can make sense of what is otherwise senseless. In similar terms, the dream, after psychoanalytic interpretation, loses its immediate character of nonsensical imagery and is understandable as a compromise formation which gives distorted expression to an unconscious wish.

Now there is a serious problem with Freud's pedagogic strategy. In all three sets of examples Freud represents slips of the tongue as resulting from two mutually interfering purposes. In the third case, however, the inferred unconscious purpose differs from the consciously acknowledged purposes of the first two only in respect of being unconscious. But this may give the impression that unconscious processes are homogeneous with conscious ones. All the categories employed to describe conscious mental acts – ideas, purposes, resolutions, intentions, etc. – can be applied to the unconscious processes; the only respect in which the latter differ from the former is the absence of consciousness.

However, the developed import of Freud's investigations into the nature of unconscious processes is that they are radically different from conscious processes. More specifically for Freud, the laws governing the two sets of processes differ radically. In the famous remark of Freud's biographer, Ernest Jones:

Careful students of Freud have perceived that Freud's revolutionary contribution to psychology was not so much his demonstrating the existence of the unconscious, and perhaps not even his exploration of its content, as his proposition that there are two fundamentally different kinds of mental processes, which he termed primary and secondary respectively, together with the description of them. The laws applicable to the two groups are so widely different that any description of the earlier one must call up a picture of the more bizarre kinds of insanity.[1]*

That the real disjunction to be found in Freud's work is not so much that between conscious and unconscious as primary versus secondary processes is important for the following reason. Freud's concern to demarcate two sets of heterogeneous processes leads him to adopt a systematic description and speak of 'the unconscious'. More correctly, Freud adopts the abbreviations *Ucs.*, *Pcs.* and *Cs.* to designate the hierarchy of psychical systems to which processes belong. A conventional philosophical criticism of Freud is that his principal errors derive from this appending of the definite article and the move from the merely adjectival or adverbial to the substantive use of 'unconscious'. The major force of such criticism comes from the erroneous belief that Freud thinks of the unconscious as a 'second mind' which reasons, forms resolutions and entertains beliefs. In other words, Freud is accused of duplicating the mind of which we are immediately aware with an unconscious analogue which differs only in being unconscious. It is clear that Freud did no such thing. He is concerned to understand the whole of the personality as a systematic relationship between two irreducibly heterogeneous sets of psychic processes each governed by radically different laws.

Freud's conception of this psychic apparatus has its roots in his earliest research and, more specifically, the 1885 *Project for a Scientific Psychology*. In this, Freud attempted to supply a complete neurological theory of the mind's workings. In abandoning this attempt, Freud gave up trying to state psychological facts in neurological terms, or map psychical functions on to a neurological apparatus. Nevertheless, what clearly survived throughout Freud's subsequent work was a certain *model* of the mind, albeit one whose physiological commitments ostensibly were suspended.

What are the important features of this model? At its perceptual end, the psychic apparatus is open to the external world. All ideas, or presentations, arise as perceptual registrations of the world and its

---

* Superior figures refer to the Notes at the end of each chapter.

objects, and are automatically stored as memory traces of those original presentations. From the somatic end of the psychic apparatus arise instinctual drives which thereby supply the apparatus with its internal energy and motion. Freud can thereby claim to supplement his 'topographical' interpretation of the apparatus with 'dynamic' and 'economic' ones. For Freud, the apparatus is not simply differentiated, topographically, into distinct 'sites' or systems, and psychic phenomena are not simply to be classified according to the place they occupy within the apparatus. There is a set of forces specific to each system, and psychic phenomena can be understood, dynamically, as resulting from conflicts between these forces. These, in turn, can be seen in economic terms to derive from quantifiable distributions of instinctual energy within the apparatus as a whole.

The drives originally seek satisfaction through an external object. Thereafter, they seek discharge through the psychic presentation of that object. As a theory of the *psychic*, psychoanalysis is concerned to deal not with drives in biological terms but with their representatives in the psyche. For the most part then, Freud is careful to distinguish between the physiological notion of an instinct and the properly psychical concept of an instinct's psychical representative. This latter is said to consist of its idea, or presentation, and a certain quota of psychical energy, or 'affect'. The primary process is said to be governed by the pleasure principle which means that there is an uninhibited flow of wishful impulses subject only to the avoidance of unpleasure and the procuring of pleasure. The primary processes are further said to be unchecked by logical contradiction, causal association or sense of time.

The secondary processes, on the other hand, are governed by the reality principle which ensures that the search for satisfaction of a wish is conducted according to the conditions imposed by the outside world. At its simplest, repression means that a wishful impulse cannot be acknowledged by consciousness; nor, given the governance of the reality principle, can there be any normal attempt to fulfil it by action on and in the external world.

Yet the impulse seeks discharge and by the most direct route possible. This is ultimately because of the constancy principle, perhaps the most important postulate underpinning Freud's model of the psychic apparatus. This states that the mental apparatus functions so as to reduce tension, experiencing an accumulation of tension as pain, and a reduction of tension, or discharge, as pleasure. While the idea, or presentation, of a wish may remain excluded from consciousness, its energy charge will flow from this idea to other associated ideas until access to consciousness, and discharge, is secured. The eventual fulfilment of the wishful impulse, if this is repressed, is thus a disguised or distorted one. It is the associative derivatives of the originally repressed presentation that seek entry into consciousness. They succeed in proportion to their associative distance from, or degree of distortion of, this original presentation. In this sense, the symptom is the 'return of the repressed': the disguised (attempted) fulfilment of an originally repressed wish.

Let us adopt an example of neurotic behaviour to illustrate these points. It occurs during Freud's celebrated analysis of the 'Rat Man'.

One day when he was away on his summer holidays the idea suddenly occurred to him that he was too fat (German '*dick*') and that he must *make himself slimmer*. So he began getting up from table before pudding came round and tearing along the road without a hat in the blazing heat of an August sun. Then he would dash up a mountain at the double, till, dripping with perspiration, he was forced to come to a stop. . . . Our patient could think of no explanation of this senseless, obsessional behaviour until it suddenly occurred to him that at that time his lady had also been stopping at the same resort; but she had been in the company of an English cousin, who was very attentive to her and of whom the patient had been very jealous. This cousin's name was Richard, and, according to the usual practice in England, he was known as *Dick*. Our patient, then, had wanted to kill this Dick.[2]

The 'Rat Man' has an unconscious wish for the death of Richard. The idea is repressed and cannot therefore be acknowledged. Nor, given the reality principle, can there be any straightforward (attempted) satisfaction of it. The wishful impulse is thus redirected on to a surrogate which is associatively related in some way to its original presentation. In this particular instance, the relation is given by the homophony of the cousin's name and 'fat'. There can, as a result, be activity aimed at achieving this surrogate, in an attempt to secure satisfaction of the now disguised wish – in the case of the 'Rat Man', getting rid of 'fat'.

The unconscious wishful impulse would appear to possess both an automatic tendency to seek discharge or satisfaction, and a remarkably distinctive means of so achieving its end. For, although the associative paths which the unconscious wish traverse are 'forced and far-fetched', disregarding laws of causal association, they do make elaborate use of certain features of language. One of Freud's earliest intuitions was that the 'verbal idea and not the concept dependent upon it' is 'the point at which the repressed breaks through'.[3] This intuition is sustained throughout Freud's writings – but, it is fair and important to add, not in a wholly consistent manner. For the purposes of certain 'linguistic' readings of Freud *all* relations between unconscious wish and conscious phenomenon are explicable at the level of the 'verbal idea and not the concept dependent upon it'. However, there are a significant number of cases in which the relationship *is* explained at the level of the 'dependent concept'. This is so where there are perceived visual similarities between the unconscious idea and its conscious substitute – most famously in the case of objects which resemble the male or female genitals. Indeed, it is such examples which inform the most widely known version of 'Freudian symbolism'. Certainly, in many such cases the relationship is reinforced by a verbal connection (one has only to think of the English colloquial use of 'tool'). However, this need not always obtain and, where the additional linguistic relation does operate, this may well derive from a prior similarity.

If we return to the 'Rat Man' case, we can see that the connection between unconscious wish and behaviour is effected by a simple pun. However, this case may fairly be described as mild in comparison with the linguistic sophistication said to be displayed by the unconscious in many other celebrated instances. The displacement or redirection of wishes in this form and along such lines can hardly accurately be described as automatic. There is, in other words, a very real tension in Freud's explanatory model between the quasi-mechanistic language of psychic forces and the interpretative language of disguised meaning and symbolization – between, in the suggestive phrase of one critic, hermeneutics and energetics.[4]

In one sense, Freud's analysis reveals what the 'Rat Man''s draconian slimming programme really meant to him, although he himself was unable, by virtue of its disguised symbolization, to recognize his actual unconscious wish. In another sense, his action is causally explained by the automatic and mechanical redirection of pure psychic energy along certain paths. The wish itself is thus presented as an amalgam of unthinking energy and self-symbolizing intent. One's unease with such an account is only increased by many of Freud's elaborations.

In a coda to his 1915 paper, 'The Unconscious', Freud argues for a distinction within the psychical idea between thing- and word-presentation, deriving from perceptual and aural memory traces respectively: i.e., in crude terms, perceiving the thing and hearing it named. Their dissociation and the aural proximity of two word-presentations permits the punning characteristic of neurotic symptom formulation, well exemplified in the 'Rat Man' case. The distinction between word- and thing-presentation has its roots in Freud's earliest writings on aphasia, but is only tentatively advanced within the 1915 paper to provide a criterion whereby conscious and unconscious ideas may be distinguished. However, as it stands, the distinction appears a rather clumsy attempt to combine a purely mechanistic account of symptom formation with an intentional one. There are awkward questions to be answered: who, or what, 'hears' the homophony or assonance of word-presentations? Under what conditions, and for what reasons, are a word- and thing-presentation connected together as presentations of 'the same thing'? What does it mean to say that they are disconnected or dissociated?

In general terms, Freud is uncomfortable with problems associated with knowledge and meaning. For instance, he appears undecided about what might be termed the cognitive status of primary processes. He oscillates between seeing primary processes as prior to secondary processes in an order of individual genesis and in an order of archaism. At one point he insists that the term 'primary' was deliberately adopted to give an indication of their chronological priority. The primary processes are present in the mental apparatus from the first; consisting of wishful impulses they constitute the core of our being. It is only the belated subsequent appearance of the secondary processes which supplies the person with the conceptual apparatuses necessary for dealing with the external world. It is left unexplained how exactly secondary processes 'grow out' of primary processes.

Elsewhere a different view is advanced, albeit tentatively. Here 'primary' has the sense, not of prior, but of 'primitive'. Primary processes are cognitive, yet in an archaic, basic and pre-logical form. 'The unconscious' is pre-linguistic, but 'speaks' a primitive, poetic language of associations and tropes which somehow 'escapes' the constraints of formal logic. Freud appealed to the work of Karl Abel on 'primal words' in confirmation of this fundamental characteristic of primary processes. As the latter are said to ignore logic, so such primitive languages were able to express antithetical meanings by the same word. Abel's research has been shown to involve etymological mistakes. More seriously, there is a sense in which it is incoherent to suggest, without further explanation, that the same word can express two opposed meanings. A single phoneme may function so as to communicate two, or more, distinct senses – for example, 'plan'. However, it must be possible separately to indicate these different senses by accompanying gesture, verbal context, clarificatory synonyms or definitions, and so on. Crudely put, if a language comprehends a distinction between meanings, its user is able to express it, and it is not so much that one word has two meanings as that one phoneme expresses two different words.

A somewhat similar confusion on Freud's part concerns the claims made for 'negation'. 'The unconscious' may indeed say 'no' when it means 'yes', but this is quite distinct from the claim that 'no' means exactly the same as 'yes'. To misleadingly use the former, instead of the latter which is appropriate, already involves a recognition of negation and affirmation as contrary judgements which fall under distinguishable and distinct signs.

There is an important difference between saying that 'the unconscious' is illogical and that it is alogical. If 'the unconscious' consists of thoughts, these may indeed be contradictory. But this is an unexceptional fact. No person can claim perfect formal consistency between all his or her ideas. To state that 'the unconscious' is exempt from the law of contradiction is perhaps only to imply that it does not think and that its activities are not formulable as propositions. Either 'the unconscious' simply thinks in bizarre ways, or it is inappropriate to use 'thinking' to describe its activity. Freud does not resolve this ambiguity, and primary', subsequently, is expected to convey the senses of both pre-cognitive and proto-cognitive.

It can only be reiterated that such difficulties are not removed by the attempt to account for symbolic and meaning-bestowing functions in the mechanical terms of psychic energy alone. The technical term, 'psychic energy', and its associated vocabulary of 'flow', 'discharge', etc., along with the postulate of the constancy principle, have their source in the early neurological research. It is thus conventional among philosophical critics of Freud to lay responsibility for his mechanistic sins at the door of the *Project*. Of course, it is one thing to argue that neurophysiological explanation provided Freud with a model of the psychic, but quite another to imply further that the latter should be discounted by virtue of its intellectual origins. A response to the second claim might be that, though Freud's primary secondary processes distinction was suggested by neurological study, its justification can be found independently of such study. However, this defence of Freud requires further argumentation to show that the model is, in its own purely psychological terms, both coherent and supported by the evidence.

Unfortunately, Freud's own work is unhelpful in this respect. Despite the bold promise of remaining upon psychological ground, Freud frequently slips back into the language of neurology – the psychic and the central nervous system are occasionally carelessly employed as synonyms. There can be little doubt that, in hoping for an eventual integration of his psychological theory with neurology, Freud's ambition was fundamentally reductionist. In a famous phrase Freud announced that 'our psychical topography has *for the present* nothing to do with anatomy; it has reference not to anatomical localities, but to regions in the mental apparatus wherever they may be situated in the body'.[5] Freud's emphasizing of the words 'for the present' is not without significance. He occasionally anticipated the eventual redescription of psychical functions in neuroanatomical terms by citing biological facts as implicit confirmation of his psychological model. The infamous spatial 'metaphors' – behind, above, below – which purport only to designate the regular order of psychic functions are often more than metaphors.

It is important, at this stage, to clarify what Freud is being accused of. Much of the foregoing might suggest that causal and intentional accounts of human behaviour, being incompatible and inconsistent one with another, are mutually exclusive. Indeed, a presupposition once favoured within the philosophy of mind states that it is impossible to describe a voluntary action as both caused by an antecedent state of affairs and as done intentionally or for a reason. However, this idea has, over recent years, been subject to sustained criticism.

Moreover, the point being made here is a different one. In so far as Freud's causal explanations of behaviour are plausible, their plausibility derives, in the last analysis, from conceiving of the human person as a neurophysiological entity driven by purely physiological or biological processes. In so far as the intentional explanations are plausible, their plausibility derives, in the last analysis, from conceiving of the human mind as a purely psychic entity, motivated to speak and act in certain ways because of certain conscious and unconscious desires, beliefs and ideas.

Freud, and crucially his interpreters, have never made clear how his theory of mind is to be understood. Most critics are uncomfortable with a reductionist materialism, wherein the conscious and unconscious mind is taken to be simply a neurological entity. However, they remain, on the whole, ambiguous between committing Freud to a full-blown dualism and reading him in terms of a 'neutral' language, that is one which does not beg the question in favour of either dualism or materialism. The problem is that some of Freud's most important explanatory terms, ones which give his theory its overall coherence and plausibility, cannot easily survive the perpetuation of this ambiguity. For instance, if terms like 'energy', 'tension', 'mnemic trace' are understood as having purely psychic referents, then much of the cited evidence in favour of their existence and concerning their mode of functioning must be discounted. At the same time, these terms cannot, given the specific contexts in which they are employed, be consistently thought of as belonging to a 'neutral' language.

The postulate underpinning Freud's dynamic model of mind is the constancy principle. This permits an ascription of 'purposiveness' to the workings of the primary processes. Yet this is successful only to the extent that the principle is not strictly translatable into a thesis about irreducibly psychic processes. It is fair to comment that many Freudian commentators subscribe, albeit implicitly, to the dualist reading. They then take as read the neurophysiological theses which supply the Freudian model of mind with its dynamism. The mechanisms whereby these initial drives become articulated as forms of behaviour are interpreted in psychic terms. Unfortunately, such an approach leaves unanswered a number of embarrassing questions, such as how somatic instincts are 'represented' in the psyche, or, how *psychic* energy can 'flow' from idea to idea. In sum, many of the difficulties in Freud's theory of 'the unconscious' derive not from his use of two epistemologically inconsistent forms of explanation, but from two ontologically incompatible philosophies of mind. Freud's explanations are ambiguous because their object is ambiguously described.

There is a further, quite distinct, methodological problem. Freud's model is concerned to emphasize the heterogeneity of conscious and unconscious or primary and secondary processes. But it equally seeks to show individual behaviour as resulting from the conflict between, or convergence of, these two processes, rather than their operation in mutual independence of one another. This raises a problem of verification. Freud is obliged to argue that unconscious processes only become cognizable under the conditions of neurosis and dreaming. Conscious experiences or behaviour – be they dreams, slips or symptoms – are, of necessity, all that the psychoanalytic investigator has got immediately to go on. Now an unconscious wish or idea becomes known to us only by being subjected to a degree of distortion or disguise which renders it acceptable to consciousness. Thus, it is not just that Freud's inference of the unconscious is indirect; it is that the experience or behaviour from which we infer the unconscious thought is taken to be none other than the latter's disguised representation of itself to consciousness.

The problem is well illustrated by Freud's ambiguous characterization of condensation and displacement. If we think of the reported dream, slip of the tongue, omission or neurotic symptom as translating an unconscious content then, for Freud, this translation is effected through two processes. The conscious phenomenon is a condensed version of its unconscious correlate; several elements of the latter may find themselves represented in a single element of the former. At the same time, the conscious manifestation displaces the centre of emphasis and interest of the unconscious content; with the dream, key elements of its latent content may be represented by peripheral or unimportant aspects of the reported content. Now, on the one hand, condensation and displacement are viewed by Freud as essential modes of functioning of unconscious processes; on the other hand, they appear to be seen as means whereby the censor distorts unacceptable unconscious thoughts, thereby making possible the latter's entry into consciousness. In other words, condensation and displacement are viewed as either a result of the censor's action on unconscious thoughts or a property of unconscious thoughts that coincidentally secures their avoidance of censorship. Freud artlessly remarks that, if condensation is not an effect of censorship, the latter in any case benefits by it. By definition, the ambiguity cannot be resolved. Unconscious thoughts only reveal themselves on conditions acceptable and subject to the censorship of consciousness. We have no way of knowing whether or not an unconscious thought was condensed *before* it entered consciousness.

Freud's description of unconscious processes is thus problematic in two ways: first, in terms of the actual descriptions he does offer; and second, in terms of the very claim to be able to offer any description at all. These points are important since, as has been seen, the development of Freud's theory is marked by precisely a shift from the mere inferring of unconscious processes to the distinctive, if speculative, characterization of these processes. Freud's early arguments to demonstrate the legitimacy of using the word 'unconscious' had a limited, and largely uncontentious, function. The experiential evidence of consciousness suggested the need to infer other acts or processes which are unconscious and fill the gaps in the posited continuum of the psyche. 'Unconscious' was used initially in a descriptive fashion: it was merely the contrary to the property of those psychic processes which are experienced as 'conscious'. The progress of Freud's research showed 'unconscious' to be more than a mere property, and to have, in his own words, an index-value. That is, 'unconscious' came to be regarded as a sign that a given psychic process or act, in being unconscious, possessed other and more important characteristics. These latter differed so significantly from those co-attendant attributes of conscious processes as to oblige Freud to adopt a systematic use of the concept 'unconscious' and to speak of different psychic systems, to which conscious and unconscious processes respectively belong.

'Conscious' and 'unconscious' designate heterogeneous and conflicting systems. The unconscious is not regarded by Freud as *another*, second, consciousness, it is fundamentally *other* than, though determinant of, consciousness. In claiming that there is an unconscious, Freud does not employ evidence for the existence of a separate, reasoning mental agency in each of us. Rather, the existence of real, psychically efficacious processes of a radically different nature from those of which we are immediately aware must be inferred from the very evidence of the latter.

Ironically, the first systematic topography of *Ucs.*, *Pcs.* and *Cs.* was eventually displaced by that of Id, Ego and Super-Ego in which the term 'unconscious' reverted to its original and descriptive function. In the earlier work Freud had been concerned above all with the facts of repression, and the repressed idea was easily conceived of as the prototype of the unconscious. Of course, the fact of repression meant that some mental agency had to be presumed responsible for the original, and then continued, exclusion of the idea in question from consciousness. The ego was given this function and Freud simply assumed that the provinces of the system consciousness and ego overlapped.

However, one fact in particular made it difficult to maintain this correspondence and thereby reconcile the systematic use of the term, 'consciousness', with its descriptive meaning. This was the fact, long recognized by Freud, that the repressing agency was unconscious, but not all that is unconscious is repressed. An important part of the ego remains unconscious. In other words, the systematic antithesis of consciousness and unconscious had to be replaced by one between the ego and the repressed.

Freud's belief that there were ego instincts combining the functions of repression and self-preservation, and his researches into the phenomenon of narcissism, led him to a classification of the instincts and a characterization of the ego which make the second topography significantly different from the first. The opposition of id and ego is not equivalent to that of consciousness and the unconscious. Of course, the concept of the id is, in many ways, the theoretical heir to that of the system, *Ucs.*, sharing as it does its most important features, those of the primary process. But this only serves to reinforce the central point at issue. The systematic use of the term 'unconscious' arose precisely because the mere designation of a mental process as unconscious had no necessary explanatory force. What was important was not so much whether an idea was conscious or unconscious, but whether it could be characterized in various other ways. To the extent that these – for instance, subjection to the pleasure principle, participation in the primary process – followed from being unconscious, Freud felt justified in using the systematic term, 'the unconscious'. However, once the systematic opposition within the psyche was misleadingly characterized as one between conscious and unconscious, Freud adopted a new nomenclature. The term 'unconscious' reverted in large part to its original descriptive function, and its 'index-value' lost importance besides that of being a 'property'.

Freud set out initially to demonstrate that there are many ideas of which we are unaware but which nevertheless play a crucial role in explaining those ideas of which we are aware. The iceberg metaphor seems appropriate here. The greater, and more important, part of ourselves is hidden from conscious view. But nothing in this metaphor would suggest that 'the unconscious' is composed of anything other than much more of the same 'stuff" – ideas, thoughts, beliefs, intentions – of consciousness, albeit below the surface of awareness. Once Freud gained an understanding of the working of unconscious processes, and their asymmetrical relation to conscious processes, he conceived of 'the unconscious' and 'consciousness' as heterogeneous, yet interrelated, systems of the same mind. Subsequently, the 'conscious'/'unconscious' disjunction was seen to be inappropriate as a description of this systematic opposition, and eventually another topology was introduced.

The developed Freudian model of mind may indeed be incoherent. However, this cannot entirely be the result of his use of the terms, 'unconscious' and 'the unconscious'. These latter do not adequately summarize Freud's work. Moreover, the real difficulty with the model lies not in the purported existence of two minds, but in the explanations given of how the two systems, constituting the same mind, interact. As has been argued, such explanations combine uneasily the languages of intentionality and mechanical causality. And, while nothing might preclude the use of both languages to describe the same events, there is a real problem when the respective explanatory languages derive from different, and radically incompatible, characterizations of the events in question. These points can be made in a different form, and one which offers a summary of Freud's professed achievement.

Freud's claim was to have effected a Copernican revolution. As the Copernican theory displaced man's planet from the centre of the universe, so Freud's explanatory model purports to displace consciousness from the centre of mind. Some enigmatic words of Freud will serve to illuminate this claim. In his 1915 paper Freud remarks that 'the attribute of being conscious, which is the only characteristic of psychical processes that is directly presented to us, is in no way suited as a criterion for the differentiation of systems'. Later on, he adds, 'the more we seek to win our way to a metapsychological view of mental life, the more we must learn to emancipate ourselves from the importance of the symptom of "being conscious" '.[6]

In what does this emancipation consist? At its simplest, we are reminded that though what we are immediately and certainly aware of must always necessarily serve as the methodological point of departure, such conscious data indicate their own inadequacy. We are compelled to infer the existence of unconscious mental processes whose significance is at least equal to that of conscious mental processes. Further, and more importantly, we are seriously misled if we believe that unconscious mental processes share those attributes indicated to us as defining the consciously mental. The unconscious differs from consciousness in far more than a mere absence of consciousness. Moreover, the character of conscious processes is determined by that of these inferred unconscious processes. Consequently, the attributions of meaning we consciously make to our experiences and behaviour are doubly inadequate. We cannot know, or be certainly aware of, the sense of our utterances and actions, since we cannot, by definition, be aware of the unconscious processes which cause us to say and do certain things, and in any case we cannot, by means of the logic of conscious ratiocination, adequately grasp the dislogic of unconscious desire.

Clearly then, the Copernican revolution of Freud involves more than simply a denial of Descartes's identification of conscious and psychic. But, equally clearly, Freud is not simply redefining the psychic as an unconscious mind in addition to the conscious mind. Freud's human being possesses an unconscious, not as a second mind, but as the unthinking and desirous core, formative of all that the person is consciously aware of saying and doing. The extent to which this theory can be rendered coherently depends ultimately on how Freud's human being is conceived in relation to Descartes's other legacy – dualism.

Notes

1   E. Jones, *Sigmund Freud, Life and Work*, vol. I (London 1945), p. 436.
2   S. Freud, *The Standard Edition of the Complete Psychological Works of Sigmund Freud*, edited by J. Strachey (London 1953–73) (hereafter *SE*), X, pp. 188–9.
3   S. Freud, *The Origins of Psychoanalysis: Letters of Wilhelm Fliess, Drafts and Notes, 1887–1902*, edited by M. Bonaparte, A. Freud and E. Kris (New York 1954), p. 242.
4   P. Ricoeur, *Freud and Philosophy: An Essay in Interpretation*, translated by D. Savage (New Haven and London 1970), especially Book 2, Part 1.
5   'The Unconscious', *SE*, XIV, p. 175.
6   ibid., p. 192 and p. 193.

Further reading

The central text for Freud's views on the unconscious is clearly the great 1915 paper, 'The Unconscious' (*SE*, XIV, pp. 159–215), but, given the importance of this notion to his work and its relation to other key concepts, all of his writing needs to be taken into account. Useful in this respect is the *Abstracts of the Standard Edition of the Complete Psychological Works of Sigmund Freud* (edited by Carrie Lee Rothgeb, New York 1973). On the whole, the *Introductory Lectures on Psychoanalysis* (1915–17) and *New Introductory Lectures on Psychoanalysis* (1932) provide clear and accessible introductions to the early and late views on Freud. A short, clear and confident statement of the early views can also be found in the 1909 *Five Lectures on Psycho-Analysis*, reprinted in *Two Short Accounts of Psycho-Analysis* (London 1962).

Useful short exegeses of Freud are Richard Wollheim's *Freud* (London 1971) and O. Mannoni's *Freud: The Theory of the Unconscious* (London 1971). A marvellous guide to the technical terminology of psychoanalysis, heavily influenced by Lacan's work, is J. Laplanche and J. B. Pontalis, *The Language of Psycho-Analysis* (London 1980).

For a critique of Freud's notion of an unconscious language without contradiction, as well as other extremely perceptive remarks on language and psychoanalysis, see Emile Benveniste's 'Remarks on the Function of Language in Freudian Theory', in his *Problems in General Linguistics*, translated by M. E. Meek (Miami 1971).

An influential critique of Freud's notion of the unconscious from within the tradition of analytic philosophy is A. C. MacIntyre's *The Unconscious: A Conceptual Analysis* (London 1958). MacIntyre's account underplays the primary–secondary processes distinction to the benefit of a certain 'second mind' interpretation. A useful corrective to this approach is given in R. S. Peters's *The Concept of Motivation* (London 1958), and in a critical review of much analytical philosophy writing on the unconscious by G. Boudreaux, 'Freud on the Nature of Unconscious Mental Processes', *Philosophy of the Social Sciences*, **7** no. 1 (March 1977), pp. 1–32.

An excellent and varied collection of philosophical writing on Freud can be found in R. Wollheim and J. Hopkins (eds.), *Philosophical Essays on Freud* (Cambridge 1982).

2

Sartre's critique

The enormous importance of Freudianism in contemporary French intellectual life owes much to the work of Jacques Lacan, which will be considered in Chapter 3. A central target for Lacan was a French philosophical tradition which rejected the Freudian notion of 'the unconscious', and whose most notable representative was Jean-Paul Sartre. While Sartre's critique of Freud owes much to his own 'phenomenological existentialism', it was also influenced by George Politzer's *Critique of the Foundations of Psychology*, first published in 1928. Regrettably, Politzer's work is now comparatively neglected. It is thus worth briefly examining its arguments before turning to the work of Sartre himself.

Politzer was concerned to rescue and restate the truly valuable in Freud's discoveries, while totally rejecting its theoretical underpinnings. Politzer's stated commitment was to what he called a concrete psychology. For him, this entailed understanding all psychic acts as having their meaning only within the concrete drama of the first person. Politzer claimed that the young Freud's insights accorded well with such a notion of concrete psychology, but that his later theoretical metapsychology betrayed them. In particular, Politzer levelled against the Freudian notion of the unconscious two interrelated charges – those of *abstraction* and *realism*. These terms are Politzer's own and since, in their normal Anglo-American philosophical usage, they have different connotations, they should be understood within the context of Politzer's arguments.

In his early understanding of dreams formation Freud, according to Politzer, was able successfully to show how an individual dream had meaning as the realization of a desire. This latter was firmly rooted within concrete individual experience. In the metapsychological account of dreams, however, the individual desire is replaced by a

38

general impersonal process of Desire in general. The imputed mechanisms and forces of the unconscious are described in the 'third person' and omit any mention of the concrete subjectivity which defines the proper domain of psychology. The later Freud's functional formalism falsely transposed the acts of an 'I' into the interactions and motions of impersonal psychic things.

Politzer's second charge against Freud is that of realism. Freud, according to Politzer, accorded a 'reality' to the unconscious on the basis of a certain (mis)reading of the facts. An alternative reading in terms of significative intentions obviates the necessity for any 'real' unconscious. The facts in question are those of dream interpretation which seem to provide a distinction between the manifest content of the dream – the actual narrative given by the woken dreamer – and its latent content which emerges only after analysis and interpretation.

According to Politzer, Freud incorrectly believed this distinction to correspond to, and thus confirm, a real distinction of mental agencies: consciousness and the unconscious. Freud's basic error was his presupposition that the dream possesses two contents: the manifest representing a real and distinct transformation of the latent. For Politzer, on the other hand, the dream has only one content – that which is termed latent – and the dream has this sense immediately, not subsequent to a process of disguise. Politzer summarized Freud as claiming that in dream interpretation the path traversed from manifest to latent content is the exact reverse of that involved in the very process of dream formation – the unconscious subjecting its latent wishes to a disguised form which renders them acceptable to consciousness.

Politzer claimed that the dream merely expresses, albeit in an unconventional language, the wishes of the individual. It is only what he termed the postulate of the priority of conventional thought which prompts us to seek a second true meaning of the dream below its manifest expression. Because this latter is inadequate to its actual sense, and given his postulate, we seek a conventional rendering of this sense in a second content. Politzer insisted that the true relation of manifest to latent content is one of immanent meaning. The purportedly unconscious wish, or infantile memory, is not absent from the narrated dream, only to be found in another and distinct place; it is present in, and immanent to, the dream, just as the rules of the game are present in a tennis match. Dream interpretation should not be thought of as the lifting of a veil which permits us to see a distinct and separate entity.

Our understanding of ourselves has merely been deepened by taking into account the possibility of a new relation, albeit an unconventional one, between expression and meaning.

The need to introduce a notion of the unconscious proceeds from the inadequacy of any possible conscious account to the meaning of the behaviour in question. However, it was simply misleading to institute an unconscious, and then to project into it what the account lacks in order to be adequate. Instead, this inadequacy of meaning should be understood in terms of an individual's dialectic of signification, that is, the concrete drama of the first person. Politzer accepted that the individual subject is an unfavoured position with respect to a possible objective understanding of the meaning of his own actions. However, this opacity or ignorance is unremarkable and certainly does not license the introduction of any concept of an 'unconscious'. The 'facts' of the unconscious are not immediately given, but constructed on the basis of certain unstated and unproven postulates. The error is only compounded when such a reified unconscious is further abstracted from the concrete domain of first person subjectivity and filled with impersonal mechanisms.

There is nothing in Sartre's work to compare with Politzer's concise and elegant treatment of Freud. Indeed, within Sartre's massive output explicit references to and discussions of Freud occupy surprisingly little space – though their content has a disproportionate significance. In general terms, Sartre's intellectual relationship with Freud was ambiguous. An explicitly stated admiration for Freud's achievements combined with a philosophical repudiation of Freudian theory. Sartre spoke once of the intellectual shock he experienced as a student on passing from what he termed the atmosphere of Cartesian rationalism into his first reading of Freud's *Psychopathology of Everyday Life*; with characteristically idiosyncratic audacity he also once cited his reading of Freud, Kafka and Joyce as having helped lead him to Marxism. Such was his admiration of Freud that in 1958 Sartre accepted John Huston's commission of a screenplay for the latter's projected film biography. The eventually released 1962 film did not have Sartre's name among its credits. His seven- to eight-hour script was, not surprisingly, unacceptable to both Huston and his American producers. Sartre's comments on the rejected screenplay reveal his profoundly held beliefs about all exemplary thinkers: namely, that a great intellectual is one who, in the midst of and living through an experience, is able to uncover its true meaning. Freud, for Sartre, was the exemplary thinker *par excellence*.

Of more direct importance than this personal admiration was Sartre's explicit insistence, throughout the late 1950s, that Marxism should open itself up to the challenge of Freud and psychoanalysis. Sartre had in mind a fertile combination of the psychoanalytic investigation of the meanings of individual experiences with a Marxist illumination of the social, historical and cultural context of such experiences.

All of this might appear to confirm Sartre's claim to have been a critical fellow-traveller and not a 'false friend' of Freudian psychoanalysis. However, besides the stated admiration must be set Sartre's vigorous and repeated denials of Freud's most central claims. Indeed it is hard to imagine a more obvious incompatibility than that between Sartrean existentialism and Freudian psychoanalysis. The starting point of the former is an analysis of 'consciousness'. Building on the phenomenology of Husserl, Sartre presented intentionality both as the sole defining mark of consciousness and in ontological terms. That is, for Sartre, consciousness is always necessarily consciousness *of* something, this latter understood as distinct from and independent of, consciousness. As a result, consciousness is emptied of content and defined as a pure and free spontaneity. It is, for Sartre, an 'illusion of immanence' to conceive of consciousness as some sort of container, wherein images, ideas, impressions, etc., are to be found. Sartre is thus sharply critical of any description of a desire, for instance, as being 'in' consciousness. A given desire is nothing but an intentional structure of the whole consciousness, a consciousness of these objects as desirable. In each of its intentional structures, consciousness is unitary. There is nothing left over, behind or beneath this consciousness. On these grounds alone any notion of an unconscious is unintelligible.

In addition, Sartre criticizes Freud's idea of the communication in radical separation of unconscious and conscious. How can an unconscious idea, of which consciousness can, by definition, have no inkling, come nevertheless to play a role in behaviour and speech of which there is consciousness?

Let us assume the existence of an unconscious desire which constitutes the true meaning of, or reason for, a given action. In Chapter 1 a simple example from the 'Rat Man' case illustrated just such a possibility. His compulsive slimming programme was explained by an unconscious desire to get rid of the intrusive Richard. The individual concerned has no awareness or even suspicion of such a desire when s/he acts in the ways s/he does. S/he has no access to the true explanation of his or her behaviour since this lies in a desire radically separate from his or her consciousness. Now a psychoanalyst may correctly conjecture the existence of the desire which explains the individual's behaviour. The individual may concur in this hypothesis. S/he does so because, while none of the desires or motives of which s/he is aware satisfactorily explains his or her behaviour, the imputed unconscious desire does provide just such a satisfactory explanation. The individual's reasons for acceding to the psychoanalyst's hypothesis differ in no significant way from those whereby s/he would agree to suggested reasons for another person's behaviour. In other words, s/he stands in relation to his or her own unconscious as s/he would to another consciousness: s/he interprets him or herself in the 'third person'. The psychoanalyst merely mediates between his or her conscious self and his or her unconscious other. Indeed, it is not inconceivable, on such an account, that the individual should psychoanalyse him or herself. Adopting a disinterested stance, s/he could venture various explanatory hypotheses about his or her own behaviour until s/he found one which satisfied all the criteria of psychological explanations.

However, such an account is a simplistic rendering of Freud's teaching and Sartre recognizes as much. He might have quoted Freud's own insistence that there is an important difference between a patient merely accepting, on the basis of evidence offered, an analyst's postulation of an unconscious desire, and his or her being able to recognize and sincerely acknowledge such a desire as truly his or her own. A third-person ascription may constitute the true interpretation of a neurotic action; it is the eventual first-person avowal, if and when it occurs, which may signal the 'cure' of the neurosis.

Sartre is content to accept that, on Freud's developed account of analysis, the unconscious is not 'indifferent' to the conjectures of the analyst, but exhibits a resistance to an analysis which approaches the truth. Resistance is a conscious phenomenon in so far as the patient, in showing aggression or anxiety, will be aware of so doing. Yet resistance must also be understood as a patient's recognition, in some form and at some level, of the unconscious desire as both his or her own desire and as unconscious, that is, as having been repressed for a reason. For Sartre, it is legitimate to ask: who or what is thus disturbed and resisting analysis?

42

The unconscious wish seeks, and thus cannot resist, its own conscious expression. Consciousness itself cannot both be aware of the unconscious desire and strive to deny it. The only agency left to which the function of resistance can coherently be attributed is the censor, which, in Freud's favoured imagery, stands at the doorway or frontier between consciousness and the unconscious. The censor allows through to consciousness those ideas from the unconscious which in themselves, or through disguise, are acceptable to consciousness. However, it is the very position of the censor – straddling two radically separate psychic domains – which makes precise explication of its status difficult.

Let us adopt a Freudian analogy and consider consciousness and the unconscious as two neighbouring countries, separated by a frontier. The censor acts as immigration control. Unconscious desires seeking conscious expression are to be thought of as illegal immigrants striving to cross the frontier unnoticed. To this end, they effect disguises. Now, there are two possible explanations of how successful entry might be achieved. First, the illegal immigrants might adopt such disguises as allow them to escape the attentions of immigration control; second, they might be spotted by the control who nevertheless provides them with such disguises as allows them to escape further notice in the country entered. Of the first possibility, the following can be noted. The unconscious has, by definition, no knowledge of external reality. In terms of the analogy, the hopeful immigrants have no knowledge of the customs or habits of their neighbouring country. The ability to assume disguises which successfully take in that country's most vigilant officers means endowing the immigrants with preternatural foreknowledge of a country never previously visited. The second alternative entails only the existence of corrupt officials whose explicit allegiances are belied by their actual actions. Once the metaphor is reconverted, however, the problem of satisfactorily explaining the phenomenon of resistance appears more pressing.

As a conscious agency, the censor is aware of the psychoanalyst's interpretation; as an agency on the frontier between consciousness and the unconscious, the censor is aware of the unconscious desire which is the subject of that interpretation. As such it is able to compare the repressed desire with the psychoanalytic hypothesis aiming to disclose it. Furthermore, as the agent of resistance the censor has autonomy. It chooses what to resist and, as such, must minimally be conscious of its own activity. Sartre naturally asks what form of self-consciousness the censor can have. Aware, as frontier guard, of the unconscious desire, it nevertheless seeks, as protective agency of consciousness, not to be aware of such a desire and thereby sustain the latter's exclusion from consciousness. This can only mean that the censor intentionally lies to itself. It is aware of the unconscious desire only in order not to be aware of it.

Sartre introduced his discussion of the unconscious by noting that the psychoanalytic hypothesis appeared to offer a solution to the problem of self-deception, or 'bad faith'. This is the problem of whether, and if so how, an individual can lie to him or herself by simultaneously affirming and denying something about him or herself. Sartre is able to conclude: 'Psychoanalysis has not gained anything for us since in order to overcome bad faith, it has established between the unconscious and consciousness an autonomous consciousness in bad faith.'[1] A response on behalf of Freud to such criticism might stress that Freud himself was not unaware of problems of this sort. As was seen towards the end of Chapter 1 a major reason for Freud's replacement of his first consciousness/unconscious topography with that of id and ego was his enforced reconsideration of the ego's role. In *The Ego and the Id* Freud explicitly acknowledges that if resistance emanates from the patient's ego, then an important part of the latter must be unconscious. In other words, although all that is repressed is unconscious, not all that is unconscious is repressed. The ego, in both its repressing and resisting functions, is unconscious. Of course, Sartre could still justifiably reply that acknowledgement of a problem does not constitute its solution. For the problematic communication in radical separation between consciousness and unconscious which pertained to the whole psyche now serves to define the ambivalent character of one part of that psyche, namely the ego. For Sartre, the second topography merely shifts the problem of the first to a new location.

Sartre's critique of Freud, by means of the 'censor in bad faith', is a powerful, and celebrated argument. However, it relies upon a false disjunction, and has considerably less force than is often supposed. For Sartre, Freud's problem arises because consciousness and the unconscious exhaustively define the psychic. In order to know what unconscious desires are unacceptable, and inadmissible, to consciousness, the censor must belong to consciousness. However, Sartre's argument continues, the censor, as part of consciousness, cannot be aware of these unacceptable desires, whether they are forced back into the unconscious or effect disguised entry into consciousness. Otherwise the game is up, and the distinction between consciousness and the unconscious is lost. If the censor, as part of consciousness, knows, then, *ipso facto*, all of consciousness must know. The only solution is for the censor to be both aware and unaware of the unacceptable desire.

But there is nothing wrong in understanding the censor – or the unconscious part of the ego – to be a distinct psychic agency, acting in relative autonomy from consciousness and unconscious, or id and conscious ego. The censor could appreciate what unconscious desires were unacceptable to consciousness and, in resisting or approving, if suitably disguised, such desires, act on behalf of consciousness – without, crucially, having to divulge or reveal to consciousness the nature of these desires. Of course, given the connotations of the term 'agency', it is not easy to comprehend *why* the censor should behave in this way, or indeed *how* it can. It might, for instance, be maintained that the censor could only remain 'loyal' to consciousness and effectively discharge its role, if it shared all of consciousness's displeasure at being aware of undisguised unconscious desires. Had it such an attitude, it could not perform its role, or conversely, consciousness would cease to need a censor. A similar argument informs the popular attribution of 'contradiction' to the role of the film or literary censor. Censorship is desirable because uncensored material corrupts and depraves. In order to know what does corrupt and deprave, the censor must read or see the questionable material. If it is censorable, this is because it does corrupt and deprave, in which case the censor must have been corrupted. If the censor is never corrupted, then no material is censorable and the censor's role is superfluous. But, of course, there is nothing incoherent in presupposing that there are human beings who can know what material corrupts all humans *other than themselves* – though we would be well justified in asking where such paragons are to be found. Similarly, there is nothing incoherent in presupposing that the censor acts as a 'third agent', one whose loyalties to, and ability to act as the guardian of, consciousness are not belied by the nature of its duties. Freud's professedly 'crude' and 'inaccurate' metaphors for this agent – the watchman on the threshold, the frontier guard, the censor itself – show his unease with, and uncertainty over, its exact status as both part of and apart from consciousness. Arguably Freud makes difficulties for himself by his personification of the psychic agencies. The unconscious, censor and consciousness are depicted as self-conscious agents with purposes, motives and intentions. Even apart from the danger of infinite regress, such a view looks circular – the paradoxical behavioural attitudes of the individual are elucidated by means of the paradoxical behavioural attitudes of the homuncular censor – and thus assists Sartre's claim that one psyche can satisfactorily fulfil the role for which Freud requires three psychic personages.

Sartre is not concerned to demonstrate Freud wrong because incoherent. In showing that the censor must simultaneously be aware and unaware of a desire or idea, Sartre is not trying to refute Freud so much as to show that the Freudian censor only displays – as a homunculus – the self-consciousness characteristic of the whole Sartrean individual. What, for Sartre, is wrong with the Freudian theory is that it needlessly multiplies psychic agencies, and still leaves bad faith unexplained. A unitary consciousness in bad faith is sufficient to explain Freud's facts, and can itself be explained in Sartrean terms. Whether the latter part of this claim is true is open to doubt, but anyway beyond the scope of this chapter. What is true is that Sartre misconstrues Freudian theory – both by misunderstanding the possible role of the censor and by the suggestion that psychoanalysis offers a solution to the problem of bad faith. On the basis of the latter, Sartre is able to imply both that bad faith does exist as a problem and that it is this problem which psychoanalysis seeks and fails to explain.

Sartre does have a further criticism of Freud, and this concerns the latter's explanatory language. Sartre frequently refers to the 'mythology' of psychoanalysis, by which he understands the terminology of psychic forces drawn from physiology and biology. For Sartre, no theory couched in terms of causal mechanisms can possibly account for the significative or meaning-giving intentionalities that must underlie the connections between what is termed consciousness and the unconscious. If it is said that the repressed desire disguises itself, then surely this implies the following on the part of the desire or desiring agent: a consciousness of having been repressed, and repressed by reason of what the desire entails, and a project of disguise, that is, an intending to represent itself in some other form. How can psychic energy condense and displace itself along such lines without some comprehension of the end to be achieved and the means to achieve it?

This disjunction between explanatory relations of causality and comprehension forms the basis of Sartre's critique of Freud in *Sketch for a Theory of the Emotions*. There Sartre repeats his accord with the primary, if subsequently betrayed, intuition of psychoanalysis; namely that all psychic facts have a meaning or significance. The major concern of the psychoanalytic hypothesis is with the symptom, a conscious pheno-menon, which it sees as the symbolic realization of a desire repressed by the censor. The symptom, be it fainting, obsessional behaviour or whatever, is experienced consciously only for what it is. Yet it symbol-ically expresses the repressed desire. The symptom, in other words, is a signifier which stands for that which is signified or meant, namely the repressed desire.

As will become apparent from Chapter 3, there is some irony in Sartre's use of these particular terms. He would appear only to be employing 'signifier' as meaning 'that which represents something else' and 'signified' as meaning 'that which is represented by something else'. For Sartre, the signified (the desire represented by a symptom) and its relation to the signifier (the symptom which represents the desire) are not disclosed to the individual. The man who compulsively steals is aware only of his stealing and of his having to steal. He has no consciousness of having to steal as a means to punish himself, although the desire to do so is symbolically expressed by his acts of theft.

How are we to understand this relation of signified to signifier? Sartre sees only two possibilities. The signified may stand to the signifier in a causal relation of originating event to effect. For example, the lighting and burning of a camp fire results in a pile of ashes. These latter are the effect, and at the same time a sign of a fire having been burnt. The ashes have this signifying function, but it is only an outside observer who interprets them thus. The ashes do not understand themselves as meaning that a fire was lit and burnt. They are merely the passive, caused residue of an original event. Now if the relation between repressed desire and symptom is analagous, then consciously experi-enced phenomena have a meaning, but this is not immanent to the experience. It is caused by something outside, transcendent to, con-sciousness which is, like the ashes, merely a caused passive residue.

Sartre rules out such a possibility, not by further argument, but by a theory of consciousness which he considers to be self-evident. Sartre's point seems to be this. A causal relation can only obtain between two distinct events, one temporally antecedent to the other. Consciousness is exempt from such causality. This is because consciousness is not a thing, and does not, literally, exist within time. Rather, consciousness is a 'project' which temporalizes itself and gives meaning to its own intentional activity. One cannot, therefore, sensibly speak of distinct, temporally successive events of the same consciousness, linked by an 'external' relation of cause and effect.

Thus, for Sartre, the only possible relation between signified and signifier is an immanent bond of comprehension. The relation between symptom and repressed desire, and the constitution of the former as a sign of the latter, is, for Sartre, an 'intra-structural bond of consciousness'. Psychoanalytic theory errs profoundly in treating the relation between symptom and desire as at once one of causality and understanding. The two relations are radically incompatible. However, it is legitimate to ask Sartre the following. If consciousness constitutes the symptom in its meaning as symbol of the repressed desire, how is it that the individual is unaware of this meaning? Psychoanalysis would be unnecessary if the individual experienced his or her symptom as both a symptom in itself *and* as signifying a certain identifiable repressed desire. Perhaps rather than a bond of comprehension we should speak of one of comprehensibility in principle, for Sartre admits that, even if the signification – the relation between signifier and signified – is constituted by consciousness, it need not be 'perfectly explicit. There are many possible degrees of condensation and clarity'.[2]

How does Sartre explicate this idea of conscious unclarity? In the first instance, he employs a distinction between consciousness and knowledge. Consciousness is intentional, it is consciousness of objects other than itself. At the same time, however, consciousness is conscious of itself being conscious of objects. This self-consciousness is immediate, pre-reflective and non-cognitive. That is, consciousness does not, in its pre-reflective self-consciousness, take itself as an object for itself. On reflection, consciousness does explicitly become aware of itself as a consciousness of such and such an object. However, reflection is made possible by, and grounded in, pre-reflective self-consciousness. For Sartre, knowledge is a function of reflective consciousness and thus not co-extensive with, being 'less than', pre-reflective consciousness. In this sense, I can – indeed I must – be conscious of being conscious of something without necessarily knowing that I am so conscious, since my knowledge could only result from an explicit reflective grasping of my consciousness.

Now, it is further clear that Sartre regards reflection as a necessary but not a sufficient condition of self-knowledge. Reflection yields a total *comprehension* of consciousness, but this is not equivalent to a full conceptualized *knowledge*. Reflection may lack the 'instruments and techniques' to 'fix by concepts' the reflected-upon consciousness and thus bring it forth into the full light of day. In reflection, consciousness 'is penetrated by a great light without being able to express what this light is illuminating. We are not dealing with an unsolved riddle as the Freudians believe; all is there, luminous; reflection is in full possession of it, apprehends all. But this "mystery in broad daylight" is due to the fact that this possession is deprived of the means which would ordinarily permit *analysis* and *comprehension*.'³

Such conceptualization can only be achieved through 'the Other'. The Other is a key Sartrean concept with many connotations. In this context, the term can be understood to denote the generic category of all other human beings. Like Politzer, Sartre does not believe that the individual experiencing subject is in a privileged position objectively to understand the meaning of his or her own experiences. It is the Other who will be able conceptually to articulate such experiences, but, importantly for Sartre, these are already totally comprehended in reflection by the subject. The other – the analyst – only brings the individual to know what he already understands. This, then, is Sartre's explication of how an experience whose meaning is constituted by consciousness can nevertheless remain opaque to that experiencing consciousness. In so far as the individual is pre-reflectively conscious of his experience, that experience is unthematized – it has not been made the explicit object of a reflection. Even if thematized, the experience will be unconceptualized, for while reflection yields total comprehension, only the objective attitude of the Other makes conceptualization possible.

For Sartre the proper sense of 'latency' is not given by according reality to a psychic domain distinct from consciousness. What is latent is immediately and immanently given to consciousness, but it may be unthematized or 'inadequately' given to the subject by the standards of objective conceptual thought. There are two problems with such an interpretation – one from the side of Freud and the other from that of Sartre.

In Freud's topography of *Ucs.*, *Pcs.* and *Cs.*, the *Pcs.* precisely designates that which is implicit and present in psychic activity while not yet explicitly made an object of awareness for consciousness. The preconscious is 'unconscious' in the descriptive sense, but not in the systematic sense of sharing in the primary process. Properly it is merely 'non-conscious'. Freud did not spell out fully the implications of this part of his topography, but he did suggest on its basis the existence of two censorships. The first operates on the frontiers of the systems *Ucs.* and *Pcs./Cs.*; the 'second censorship' is placed between the *Pcs.* and *Cs.* Corresponding to the two censors is a distinction between *suppression* and *repression.* The latter denotes the radical exclusion of ideas from consciousness into the unconscious; the former designates merely a conscious expulsion of an idea from the immediate field of consciousness into the preconscious.

Now it seems clear that Sartre's pathology of bad faith, and, in general terms, his understanding of the unconscious correspond to these related notions of preconscious, suppression and the 'second censorship'. Sartre adopts the example from Stekel of women whose marital infidelity leads them to deny that they experience sexual pleasure. The pattern of distraction whereby such women avoid any conscious recognition of pleasure corresponds exactly to what Freud understands by suppression. Ironically, therefore, when Sartre cites such evidence to confirm his 'refutation' of the Freudian unconscious, he radically misconstrues the real line of division between conscious and unconscious.

Although the Freudian doctrine is introduced as a possible solution to the pathology of self-deception or bad faith, it is clear that the kind of case Sartre has in mind is marginal to psychoanalysis. Sartre does not offer a re-interpretation of the celebrated Freudian case histories, and the self-deceiving coquette or self-effacing waiter of *Being and Nothingness* are far removed from 'Little Hans' or the 'Rat Man'. As it stands, Sartre's theory is incapable of explaining the classic Freudian cases, though that, of course, should not be taken to imply that Freud's own explanations are adequate.

Sartre's theory of bad faith rests upon the possibility of a person systematically misrecognizing the meaning of his or her behaviour. It tries to capture the sense in which somebody chooses not to see something about their actions or character, of which nevertheless they are aware *at some level.* Now Freud renders the notion of 'level' by speaking of psychic regions or compartments, between two of which, the unconscious and consciousness, there is a cognitive barrier. Sartre, it seems wants to understand 'levels' in terms of a cognitive hierarchy within one and the same consciousness, and between which there is, in principle, possible transition.

The metaphors common to Sartre and Freud may help us to grasp what he is trying to argue. It is if all that is present within an individual mind would be visible if consciousness looked in a mirror. But, even when a person does look into the mirror and sees all that there is to be seen, s/he may not recognize what s/he is seeing. There is, after all, a difference between 'seeing x' and 'seeing *that* it is x'. Bad faith might be explained, in terms of the metaphor, as 'seeing x, but failing to see that it is x one is seeing'. Extending this same metaphor to Freud, his notion of consciousness becomes both seeing x and seeing that it is x; the pre-conscious is not seeing x because, although it is within one's available visual field, one is not attending to it, being distracted by, or concentrating upon, other items within the field; and, finally, the unconscious is that which cannot be seen because it is outside, excluded from one's visual field.

Sartre always denied Freud's central claim that we do not, and cannot, see all there is to be seen about ourselves, that there is something 'hidden' from our conscious gaze. For Sartre, all is there to be seen or experienced. What is 'hidden' from, or inaccessible to, us are the means to know and/or express what is already totally comprehended. Thus, Sartre's initial reinterpretation of Freudian doctrine rests upon a notion of the conceptual opacity of even reflected-upon consciousness. This 'mystery in broad daylight' is dispelled not from within, but from without through the agency of another. In *Being and Nothingness* the disjunction within consciousness lay between comprehension and knowledge. In later work Sartre speaks instead of 'lived experience' but still maintains that the process of lived experience is obscure to itself, since susceptible only of comprehension never knowledge. Lived experience is present to itself in exactly the same way that consciousness was always pre-reflectively self-conscious. However, lived experience is 'absent' from itself in so far as it cannot *name* itself, that is, find the means adequately to express itself in public language.

In *Being and Nothingness* the failure of self-knowledge was a function of the subject's position with respect to his own experiences. The later comments suggest a more fundamental 'unsayability' of experience which, in turn, indicates a general or universal gap between what can be comprehended and what can be named. What is significant about both accounts, however, is the priority accorded to the immanent and immediate translucidity of experience or consciousness. The individual is able totally to understand him or herself – s/he just cannot put it all

51

into words. In no way does Sartre conceive of language as formative of what can be experienced or comprehended as experienced. The comprehensibility of experience is pre-linguistic such that the Sartrean 'unconscious' is given not at the level of lived experience, but in and through the shortcomings of the latter's linguistic expression. For Sartre, the unconscious lies only on the outside of language.

This priority of meaningful experience is confirmed by Sartre's repeated conception of language as an instrument or mere means to an end which is comprehended prior to the linguistic act. In *What is Literature?* (1948) the prose writer is described as the man who uses words as signs to name the objects which lie beyond them. Unambiguous use of language results in the revelation of the objects themselves and the consequent effacement of the words which served only as indicators of their presence. In a 1965 interview Sartre reiterated his belief that language essentially serves as a means rather than an end. Its aspect as the latter is of importance only during that 'intermediary moment when the writer seeks the proper words, just as a painter seeks out the appropriate colours on his palette'.[4] For Sartre, language, as it were, realizes itself in and by abolishing itself as a separate instrument. It is the means to bringing forth or revealing that which is already comprehended or intended. If the project of expression is successful then that which is intended or meant stands directly before consciousness without the intermediary of the sign. Language can be used properly, or abused, and communication is successful, or fails, because there are ideas and experiences comprehensible outside language, for which the right words are or are not available on the linguistic palette, and, if the former, are or are not used.

Sartre's philosophical naïvety about language is frequently overlooked. Chiefly, this is because Sartre is, perhaps rightly, admired for his all-encompassing rationalist optimism, his sustained belief that nothing is inaccessible to human comprehension. Few critics take the time to examine just how far this conviction is sustained at its base by general and unargued assertions which, even in metaphorical translation, are hard to make sense of, and which are vulnerable to the most elementary philosophical criticism.

This chapter has tried to show how Sartre's critique of Freud is misdirected and how far his own account is a misconstrued alternative, inadequate on its own terms. There are, however, other ways in which Sartre tries to offer an alternative to Freud which should be mentioned

52

in summary. For instance, Sartre does provide a general account of human motivation quite different to that of Freud. Sartre criticizes the idea of an original libido or drive. It is attacked, on Politzerian grounds, for being an abstraction which cannot account for the concrete individualization of desire; and it is described as a psycho-biological residue which is empirically inducted rather than phenomenologically intuited. In its place Sartre offers an account of human reality in terms of the original project of being. Consciousness is revealed as both a lack of and desire for being. All individual concrete projects are but expressions or symbolic satisfactions of this original desire. It originates and motivates particular behaviours just as, for Freud, all particular drives are expressions of an original libido. For Sartre, human projects are self-contradictory. Human reality is defined by its very lack of being and cannot thus secure its ideal of becoming being. Man, in Sartre's celebrated phrase, is a 'useless' passion. Of course, whether, on Sartre's as opposed to Freud's account, individual projects are any more explicable in particular and concrete ways is open to argument. Sartre's real alternative to Freud is that provided by metaphysics instead of psychology. Sartre offers an ontological postulate, the desire for Being, in place of a biologically grounded postulate, libido. It is possible that such a 'desire for Being' could ultimately be explained in psychological or physiological terms. But it is difficult to see precisely how, and Sartre, preferring 'phenomenological intuition' to empirical research, certainly gave no indications of the way it might be done.

In the later, professedly materialist, ontology of the *Critique of Dialectical Reason*, Sartre defines human reality as arising from its primitive relation to surrounding matter as need. This is itself the negation or an original negation, or *lack*, within the human organism. Sartre sees such a primitive negativity as the true irreducible and criticizes Freud for singling out sexual need. Freud, he suggests, emphasized sexuality to the exclusion of other needs, only because certain social and historical conditions gave it prominence. In another context he might well have chosen hunger. That primitive need should assume a sexual form is dependent upon the individual as a totality, and this, in turn, is governed by certain social and historical givens. It may be fair to criticize Freud for 'sexual pantheism'. However, much depends on the extent to which Sartre's own concept of 'need' can be understood as a claim about psycho-biological individuals under material conditions of existence.

Nevertheless, Sartre did feel he could see the real basis of his accord with Freud. Both regard psychic life in all its manifestations as symbolizations or expressions of the fundamental structure of the individual; both regard the human being as a perpetual, searching, historization whose essential meaning is given by an original project; neither accepts that the individual alone is in a position to uncover this meaning for himself.

However, the accord signalled does appear hollow once full stock is taken of the real disagreements. Sartre's claim to accept the facts uncovered by Freud but to refuse the explanatory language of Freudianism cannot be sustained. Whatever reading is offered of the facts, Sartre cannot and does not take account of Freud's own insistence upon the radical heterogeneity of conscious and unconscious. He remained committed to a definition of the psychic fact which, whether as pre-reflective consciousness or lived experience, preserves a basic presence to itself. Every psychic fact involves an intentionality and immanent comprehensibility. The subject's ability to grasp and know his own intentionalities is not limited by their being intrinsically incomprehensible or determined by something other than consciousness. Rather they cannot always fully be conceptualized. The Sartrean unconscious is that which is comprehended but which escapes knowledge. The Freudian unconscious is radically other than consciousness, and Freud's individual can never fully grasp or comprehend all that s/he is or does. Despite the protestations of innocence, it is very difficult to see Sartre as anything other than an inconstant and 'false' friend of psychoanalysis.

Notes

1 J.-P. Sartre, *Being and Nothingness: An Essay on Phenomenological Ontology* (translated from the French, *L'Etre et le Néant*, 1943, and with an introduction by Hazel E. Barnes (London 1957)) (hereafter *BN*), p. 53.

2 J.-P. Sartre, *Sketch for a Theory of the Emotions* (translated from the French, *Esquisse d'une théorie des émotions*, 1938, by Philip Mairet and with a Preface by Mary Warnock (London 1962)), p. 53.

3 *BN*, pp. 570–1.

4 J.-P. Sartre, 'L'Ecrivain et sa langue', in *Situations IX* (Paris 1972), p. 82.

Further reading

A survey of French philosophical reaction to psychoanalysis and the notion of the unconscious from Politzer to Sartre is given by François H. Lapointe in 'Phenomenology, psychoanalysis and the unconscious', *Journal of Phenomenological Psychology*, **3** no. 1 (Fall 1971), pp. 5–25. George Politzer's *Critique des Fondements de la Psychologie*, originally published in 1928, has been reissued by Presses Universitaires de France, 1974.

The main sources for Sartre's views on Freud are his *Sketch for a Theory of the Emotions*, pp. 48–55 and *Being and Nothingness*, pp. 50–4 and pp. 557–75. His later views on 'lived experience' and its relation to the unconscious can be found summarized in the interview 'The Itinerary of a Thought', originally published in *New Left Review*, no. 58 and reprinted in *Between Existentialism and Marxism* (London 1974), especially pp. 35–42.

Two recent accounts of Sartre's criticisms of Freud, which touch on much of what has been covered in this chapter, are Ivan Soll, 'Sartre's rejection of the Freudian unconscious', and Lee Brown and Alan Hausman, 'Mechanism, intentionality and the unconscious: a comparison of Sartre and Freud'. Both are published in *The Philosophy of Jean-Paul Sartre*, edited by P. A. Schilpp (The Library of Living Philosophers, vol. XVI (La Salle, Illinois 1981)). A sophisticated review of Sartre's attitude to Freud which takes account of his work on Flaubert is provided by Christina Howells in 'Sartre and Freud', *French Studies*, **33** no. 2 (April 1979), pp. 157–76.

The views of Maurice Merleau-Ponty, Sartre's contemporary and fellow phenomenologist, on Freud provide an interesting contrast to those of Sartre. Merleau-Ponty's early views on Freud are to be found in his *The Structure of Behaviour* (translated from the French, *La Structure du comportement*, 1942, by Alden L. Fisher (London 1965)), pp. 176–80. Later comments, which make interesting reference to Politzer's work, occur in his *Themes from the Lectures at the Collège de France, 1952–1960* (translated by John O'Neill (Evanston, Illinois 1970)). A useful survey of Merleau-Ponty's evolving attitude towards the Freudian unconscious is given by J.-B. Pontalis, 'Note sur le Problème de l'Inconscient chez Merleau-Ponty', *Les Temps modernes*, **17** (1961), pp. 287–303.

3
The unconscious and language

In Chapter 2 it was argued that the Sartrean critique of Freud chooses to regard the unconscious as the unthematized horizon of present consciousness, that which is not reflectively grasped but which is, in principle at least, comprehensible. For Sartre, the term 'unconscious' serves only to translate that sense in which a person pre-reflectively understands something about him/herself, but is unable to formulate it conceptually. On such an interpretation, the analytic session itself must have a limited function. The analyst merely supplies the language whereby the analysand is able to express what s/he always and already understood. From a perspective wherein nothing of the meaning of a person's utterances or actions ever really escapes them, the Freudian concept of the unconscious loses its radical originality and the practice of psychoanalysis is stripped of its privileged status.

A powerful rejoinder to such an interpretation, and its consequences, arose within the French psychoanalytic movement. It maintained that comprehension of the effects of the unconscious could not be intra-subjective, but was rather intersubjective, and, in particular, located within the relationship between analyst and analysand; it insisted that language could not have the neutral instrumental role assigned to it by Sartre, but was rather the unique site for the manifestation of the unconscious. The controversial author of this counterclaim was Jacques Lacan. His declared intent of 'returning to Freud' signalled a single-minded and passionate defence of that thinker's originality. This meant an insistence upon the radical irreducibility of the concept of the unconscious and the uniqueness of the psychoanalytic situation.

Any attempt to offer a philosophical assessment of Lacan's theory which situates it by reference to other philosophical interpretations of Freud is beset by immense difficulties. These derive chiefly from the context of Lacan's work. As the Introduction showed, the theoretical arguments of psychoanalysis are inseparable from continuing institutional debates and struggles over the actual practice of analysis. These centrally concern the terms and conditions whereby anyone acquires the right to practise as an analyst. The international psychoanalytic movement knew such struggles from the very outset; in France, Lacan's own personal career provides a guiding thread through bitter and labyrinthine disputes over the form psychoanalytic training and practice should assume.

Lacan saw himself above all else as a practising analyst and had occasion to remark that the sole aim of his teaching was the training of other analysts. The adversaries for whom he reserved his deepest and most bitter polemic were not those outside psychoanalysis who misinterpreted Freud, but those insiders whose misunderstandings of Freud were, according to Lacan, related to psychoanalytic malpractices. Given Lacan's location of his own work, it is deeply ironic that, outside France, its most significant influence has been in non-psychoanalytic domains of intellectual activity.

Lacan liked to describe himself as a practising analyst – communicating his therapeutic results. He explicitly rejected any assimilation of his work to an academic discourse which might thereby offer a transmittable compendium of it. He viewed with disfavour any attempt at synoptic exposition of his work – not because of any substantive exegetical errors, but simply for falsely assuming his thought to be summarizable. He liked to think of his work as continuing explorations, aporias rather than dogmatic assertions of theoretical certainty.

Moreover, to talk about Lacan's 'writings' is misleading. Nearly all of his work took the form of oral submissions – whether to various colloquia or in the celebrated Paris seminars. We are offered the printed texts solely on the understanding that we remember their true origins. More than one critic has asked Lacan's 'readers' to hear the original speech that is crudely transcribed on the page. A philosophical commentator on Lacan appears doubly damned in advance – for daring to extract, for philosophical purposes, what is specific to the domain of psychoanalytic practice, and for assuming that what Lacan taught about this domain can be read as systematic knowledge. Again, it should be noted that, ironically, fidelity to the authentic Lacan undercuts precisely those who have sought to import 'Lacanian' ideas into non-psychoanalytic areas of academic study.

These difficulties are compounded by, and perhaps help to explain, what is most notorious about Lacan – his personal style. No one can ignore the immense difficulties faced by any reader of his work – the extravagant puns, the polysemy of central terms, the subtle and demanding allusions to literary and other works, the presupposition of much more than a working familiarity with Freud's own writings, the expository schemas and diagrams that themselves seem to defy exposition, the disjointed argumentative narratives that simultaneously and circuitously pursue several distinct themes. It is at least curious that Lacan, who fervently repeated his fidelity to Freud, should have dramatically taken leave of his master in the matter of expository style.

Unsympathetic critics of Lacan are driven by these stylistic difficulties to declare that the Emperor is naked, that no rational kernel can be discerned beneath the mystical shell. Lacan is depicted as no more than an intellectual charlatan whose pretentious verbiage serves only to cover a fundamental theoretical vacuity. On the other hand, it is unfortunately the case that those most sympathetic to Lacan pay him the dubious homage of striving to reproduce both the content of his thought and the manner of its articulation.

There are, however, those who acknowledge the powerful originality of Lacan's ideas, but regret the near impenetrable prose within which their author chose to bury them. It *is* fair to accuse Lacan of making unnecessary difficulties for even those sympathetically disposed towards his work. At the very least, moreover, his declared purpose of solely teaching other analysts appears suspect when it is manifested in a style, and, on the evidence, a professional practice, which is overbearing, if not despotic. To be sovereign master of an incommunicable truth which is dispensed on sacred tablets is not to teach and participate in a community of learning.

Lacan was disinclined to apologize for such 'failings'. Yet such justifications as are offered have a distinctly question-begging air about them. Lacan's central claim was that 'the unconscious' and language are inextricably linked. The presence of unconscious wishes and thoughts are betrayed by the ways in which a speaker uses language. It is tropes that most especially characterize the influence of the unconscious upon language. Of course, if Lacan is correct then there can be no 'innocent' or neutral use of language, one that is not determined by unconscious mental activity. This will include talking about 'the unconscious' itself. In such a situation all one can do, perhaps, is use language in a form that allows the truth about its relation to the unconscious to become evident. However, it is fallacious simply to conclude from employing a certain mode of speech that this thesis about language's relationship to a putative 'unconscious' is thereby proven. Yet there is a sense in which Lacan – and certainly some of his followers – appear to declare: 'Listen to how I speak – what I say about the unconscious and language is thereby established.'

It is interesting, in this respect, to note the radical difference in approach to language by Sartre and Lacan. Sartre, as we saw in Chapter 2, viewed language as an instrument for the communication of thoughts. His earliest literary criticism took the form of vigorous attacks on the Surrealists for what, in Sartre's eyes, was an abuse of language's proper function as such a tool. In direct contrast, Lacan was a supporter of the French Surrealist movement. It is significant also that the French Surrealists were the first champions of Freudianism in France, seeing their own art as a direct expression of 'the unconscious'. Freud himself was not inclined to agree with them.

Lacan's chosen style of expression does not just make for difficulties in understanding him. It precludes objective critical appraisal. To deny that a truth can be spoken of in rational and closed terms safeguards it only at the expense of a certain solipsism. Lacan was quick to condemn the heresies of his erstwhile disciples. But such condemnations have the air of *ex cathedra* judgements, rather than reasoned demonstrations of mistaken interpretation. If the master declares that we misunderstand him, who, or how, are we to disagree.

There is, above all, a certain disingenuousness in Lacan's claim to speak from, and solely concerning, the domain of psychoanalytic practice. Disclaimers about speaking philosophically occur in texts that make frequent and free use of philosophical sources. Lacan was certainly never unaware of the philosophical implications of his theoretical claims, and indeed was often anxious polemically to underline these. A small example: the 1949 printed text of the celebrated paper on the 'mirror-stage', in reworking the original version delivered in 1936, makes deliberate and unmistakable reference to the 'contemporary philosophy of being and nothingness'. Lacan chose to address philosophers, entering, for instance, into debate over Freud's conception of negation with the eminent French philosopher, Jean Hyppolite, and entertaining at his seminars many of the stars from Paris's peculiar intellectual constellation.

Lacan's writings are multi-layered reflections, rather than the sustained presentation of a coherent theory – and my exposition will, for better or worse, follow this pattern. Lacan's thoughts concerning the Freudian unconscious have been resumed in two celebrated statements, and a third that served to distinguish his approach from that of an errant follower – 'the unconscious is structured like a language', 'the unconscious is the discourse of the Other', and 'language is the condition for the unconscious'. These *dicta* have all the compressed appeal, and conceptual ambiguity, of other popular aphorisms. However, they serve well as focal points for an account of Lacan since they represent aspects of Lacan's most fundamental and sustained insight – that any proper appreciation and understanding of the unconscious demands an appreciation and understanding of language, and its particular science, linguistics.

If the meaning of a return to Freud is a return to the meaning of Freud, then, for Lacan, the latter can only adequately be elucidated with the retrospective benefit of insights acquired after Freud. Freud's time, and consequently Freud himself, lacked the conceptual tools, provided latterly by linguistics in particular, whereby the unique discoveries of psychoanalysis could properly be formulated. This postulated relationship between Freud and linguistics should be understood in both directions. What distinguishes Lacan from other Freudians is his linguistic reading of Freud; what distinguishes Lacan from others indebted to the science of linguistics is his Freudian understanding of language.

A necessary preface to Lacan is thus some consideration of those aspects of linguistics which he chose to adopt, and adapt, for his own purposes. Lacan pays greatest tribute to Ferdinand de Saussure whom he sees as the source of modern linguistics. Saussure's innovation was to define *language* as a system – in distinction from actual speech. From such a perspective, it can be seen that language possesses a structure which is beyond the control and consciousness of individual speakers, who, nevertheless, make use of this structure in their sensible utterances. Indeed, such speech acts are only possible because this structure is present in the mind of each speaker.

The fundamental unit of this language system is the 'sign', defined by Saussure as a double entity, uniting the 'signifier' and 'signified'. The sign unites not a thing and a name, but a concept (signified) and a sound-image (signifier). Saussure qualifies this by adding that the latter is to be understood, not as something physical (the transmitted material disturbance of air), but the 'psychological imprint'. Saussure represents the sign by means of the formula, $\dfrac{\text{concept}}{\text{sound-image}}$.

Having defined the sign, Saussure advances the principle that the sign is arbitrary. He explains this as meaning that the bond between signifier and signified is 'unmotivated' rather than 'natural'. It is at this point that the problems of interpretation start. Saussure gives as an example of such arbitrariness the fact that the concept of 'sister' is 'not linked by inner relationship' to the sound-image, *sœur*, which is its signifier in French, but says that onomatopeic words are an exception to this rule. For instance, '*bow-wow*' stands for 'dog', and this is a 'motivated' or 'natural' relationship, since the signifier suggests by imitation that which is signified.

This point, however, seems confused. The words, 'sister', '*sœur*', or indeed any language's corresponding term, have no necessary relationship, as words, with the concept of a female sibling. It is only a social convention, or rule of language, which stipulates that 'sister' stands for the idea of a sister. With equal facility, and no loss of meaning, the rules could have determined that another signifier performed this function. In this sense the union of the signifier, 'sister', with the signified, the idea of sister, is 'unmotivated' and not 'natural'. But when Saussure argues that the use of 'bow-wow' to signify a dog is 'motivated', this can only be because there is a 'natural' relationship between the sound of the word and the characteristic sound of dogs. Concepts or ideas do not bark. In other words, the 'arbitrariness' in 'sister' is in the relation between word and *concept*: the 'non-arbitrariness' of 'bow-wow' obtains between word and *thing*. Saussure's concept of the 'signified' thus seems to oscillate between meaning concept and object. Further, Saussure shows no awareness of the very many philosophical problems associated with this distinction.

'Arbitrariness' has been described so far as simply the lack of any natural relationship between signifier and signified. But Saussure intended something more by this term. A given signifier performs its particular role by virtue of its relation to all other signifiers. 'Dog', as a signifier, possesses a value because, in the vocabulary we employ, it is distinguishable, *qua* word, from 'dig', 'bog', and 'dot'. For Saussure, different languages do not merely use different sets of signifiers. Each language conceptually maps, or divides up, the world in different and specific ways. An easy and much favoured example: different languages possess different sets of colour words, between which there is no exact equivalence. The user of one language is not in the position of seeing a colour for which s/he lacks the word. Rather, the individual notices those colours between which the language they use distinguishes by means of distinct colour terms. Thus, for Saussure, a given signified in one language may have no exact equivalent in another language. Each signified is related to, and consequently comprehensible in terms of, all the other signifieds of its own language. For Saussure, there is no necessity for the world to be divided up into, and understood in terms of, this particular set of meanings. Different languages are incommensurable since they articulate and organize the world in different ways.

Saussure thus recognizes two kinds of 'arbitrariness' – the lack of a natural relationship between signifier and signified, and the lack of a natural, or essential, relationship between the sign and the world. The possibility of certain extreme interpretations of Saussure is given by combining these two theses in ways that both misunderstand Saussure's formula and exploit those ambiguities which have already been mentioned. Saussure is then saddled with the view that, since words do not have to mean what they do, they could mean anything, and further that, since reality does not have to be understood in one particular way, it must be no more than the meaning that is produced by words. In sum, 'the world of words creates the world of things'.

In the Saussurean formula for the sign, $\frac{s}{S}$, a bar (—) separates the signified from the signifier (S). This bar indicates that signifier and signified have nothing in common, that there is no 'natural' necessity that a given pair should be united in a sound-meaning couplet. However, to maintain that they are distinguishable in kind is not to say that, in any given language at any given particular moment, they are actually dissociable or separable. Their connection is 'necessary', forming an 'intimate union', by virtue of the social convention or rule which stipulates, for instance, that the word 'dog' means this kind of four-legged animal. This is not to deny that, over a period of time in the development of a language, the sense associated with a particular word may shift. This is what Saussure understood by the 'sliding' of the signifier over the signified. This, of course, did not mean that, at any given moment, a set of signifiers might be 'sliding' over its signifieds. This is certainly *not* what Saussure understood as implied by the bar in his formula, and he would have been horrified to see it so interpreted.

Saussure took great care to distinguish the senses in which a language is immutable, because its present 'law' prescribes these particular meanings for words, and yet mutable, in that this law, like any other convention, may change over time. The error is to conflate this quite proper sense of mutability with the 'could be other than it is' which characterizes the relationship, at a given moment, between signifier and signified. Some commentators on Saussure, thus, have chosen to speak of 'arbitrariness' of the sign only, not of the signifier. For communication to be at all possible, any particular unit of signifier and signified is given by the rules of language. What is arbitrary is that these units of meaning, as a particular language, should divide up the world in the way that they do.

Unfortunately, Lacan and others interpret Saussure in a radical, and radically misleading, way. They represent the bar in the Saussurean formula as a barrier dividing two parallel orders, and, by understanding the 'shifting' of one with respect to the other as a dissolution of any necessary pairings of particular signifier and signified, 'establish' the 'primacy of the signifier'. For Lacan, we find the meaning of a word not by, as it were, going down below the bar to find its corresponding signified, but rather by proceeding along the line of remaining signifiers – in an utterance or indeed in the language as a whole – to discover what sense it has. And this sense is determinable only in relation to, by virtue of its specific difference from, all the rest. 'It is in the chain of the signifier that the meaning "insists" (*insiste*) but none of its elements "consists" (*consiste*) in the signification of which it is at the moment capable.'[1]

Lacan then claims that not just meaning but reality itself is to be found within the chain of the signifier. For, by collapsing the distinction between 'the thing as it is meant' and 'the thing that is meant', Lacan can claim that it is language, as merely a set of signifiers, which 'creates' reality, the 'world of things', and then claim Saussure's authority for this view.

Lacan's argument depends upon the assumption of the 'primacy of the signifier'. Such a premiss is a misconstrual of Saussure's thought. However, two points should be made. First, Lacan's misreading of Saussure is understandable given the relative crudity and carelessness with which the latter defines the sign. There may well be no way in which Saussure can be interpreted as saying anything intelligible and original about language. Second, it is not simply that Lacan misinterprets Saussure. On its own terms, Lacan's theory of meaning is inadequate. On Lacan's account of the 'primacy of the signifier' there can be no coherent explanation of how meaning is generated and communicated. Again, it is impossible to understand what a signifier is if it can be defined only in relation to other signifiers. In short, the psychoanalytic theory of meaning proposed by Lacan fails to answer any of the requirements of such a theory as it is normally, and indeed as it must be, understood.

Lacan also owes a large debt to the work of Roman Jakobson. Jakobson claims that language is ordered around two axes. If we think of language as a menu (and remember to write the menu courses left to right, with each course's alternatives listed from top to bottom), then the construction of meaningful utterances, just like the ordering of a meal, will involve two distinct operations.

Each course in the meal involves a selection from among the available alternatives – soup or *hors d'œuvre* for example. We can read these alternatives along the vertical axis defining each course. Similarly, any particular word in a sentence is chosen from among the available alternatives, these all being connected by relations of similarity or opposition, and suspended, as it were, vertically beneath the actually selected word. I choose to say 'castle', rather than 'palace' or 'mansion', and as opposed to 'hovel'.

Successive courses are ordered in order to give a complete meal. Similarly, we construct meaningful utterances by combining different words in sequence. As we read horizontally across the menu, so, on the same axis, we combine words in a spoken chain to form a sentence. The horizontal axis relates words by their contiguity; the vertical axis relates words by their similarity or opposition.

For Jakobson, these two axes serve exhaustively to define language in its functioning. Indeed, he was concerned to explain the dysfunctional use of language, aphasia, in terms of a failure to operate along either of the two axes as defined. For each failure there could be discerned a different form of aphasia; and for each type of aphasia, the loss of a specific language function. Thus aphasiacs suffering from similarity disorder are able to operate along the horizontal, but not vertical, axis. They can find words that readily combine with the lost word, but not those which are substitutable for it. They thus offer 'jumps' for 'horse', rather than 'pony' or 'donkey'. In terms of the analogy, the aphasiac 'diner' suffering from similarity disorder is unable to choose an alternative starter and orders the main course instead. In Jakobson's (somewhat confusing) terminology, this disorder is called a loss of the *metaphoric* function of language – association by similarity.

On the other hand, those aphasiacs suffering from contiguity disorder are able to operate along the vertical, but not the horizontal, axis. They cannot thus combine words into larger syntactic units and are able only to operate by metaphoric selection. Again, in terms of the analogy, the aphasiac 'diner' suffering from contiguity disorder can only order different dishes from the *same* course on the menu. This disorder is a loss of the *metonymic* function of language – connection by contiguity.

It is as well to note that the sense Jakobson gives the terms, metaphor and metonymy, does not accord with their normal meanings. Metaphor and metonymy usually refer to figures of speech in which a name or descriptive term is transferred from one object to another, there being some relation between the two objects: of analogy in the case of metaphor, or attribute or part to the whole in the case of metonymy. Jakobson understands the metaphor/metonymy distinction in a way that is familiar to linguists as that between syntagmatic/paradigmatic relationships. A sign may relate syntagmatically to those that are present with it in a sentence, that is in a linear sequence of signs. A sign may also relate paradigmatically to those signs *not* present in the sentence, though available within the rest of language. In other words, a sign used in a particular place within the linear sequence is chosen from other signs having a similar function. As with Jakobson's metaphoric/ metonymic dimensions, both syntagmatic and paradigmatic relationships are necessary to analyse a sentence. The distance between Jakobson's and normal usage of the terms, metaphor and metonymy, can lead to misunderstanding. This is especially true of their application to the analysis of unconscious associations where, as will be seen, it is not always clear whether normal usage is being illegitimately extended or Jakobson's usage is being loosely applied.

Reading Saussure's work as establishing the 'primacy of the signifier', and adopting Jakobson's ordering of language along the axes of metonymy and metaphor provides Lacan with the essential means whereby he can offer a linguistic reading of Freud's unconscious. In compressed summary, his view is as follows: the subject's accession to the use of a pre-existing language structure coincides with the institution of his or her unconscious. This is accomplished by means of metaphor, which, in turn, is indissolubly linked to the Oedipal drama. Thereafter, the effects of the unconscious upon the subject's conscious discourse and action are to be found in, and explained in terms of, the operations of metaphor and metonymy. Our original desires pass into, and are thereby lost within, the 'chain of the signifier'. We cannot ever fully recover these desires; we can only reconstruct the metaphoric and metonymic pathways they adopted, whereby their sense was lost to us.

This is, in its bare outlines, an ontogenetic account of humans which has the form, and force, of a tragic myth – an unavoidable 'fall' and an infinitely deferred redemption. It would appear that, for Lacan, our 'fall' is in acquiring language, but then he offers no simple pre-linguistic Eden. Before speaking, the child sees – and wants – everything in terms that can admit of no distinction between self and world, inside and outside. This is what Lacan terms the Imaginary – to be understood as both a stage in human genesis, and a permanent, fundamental level of the human psyche.

The crucial experience of the Imaginary is what Lacan claimed as his earliest discovery – the 'mirror-stage'. Confronted at a certain age by an image of itself in the mirror, the child identifies with the image. The sense of identification that is relevant here is the specifically psycho-analytic one – the assumption of, and transformation of oneself in accordance with, a model provided by another. The child, in identifying with its 'other', the mirror image, doubly misrecognizes itself – by assuming itself to be its reflection, grasped as a whole, and by investing the image with attributes, full motor co-ordination, which are anticipations of its future maturation. Lest common sense object against Lacan that not every culture can provide mirrors to facilitate this development, there is corroboratory evidence to be found in the observable phenomenon of transitivism. A child will reproduce, and mimic, the behaviour of its peers to the point of identifying with the other – crying out, for instance, when the other falls, or claiming, after hitting the other, to have been hit itself.

It is improper, therefore, to speak of a pre-linguistic subject in command, because fully cognizant, of itself. The Imaginary is characterized precisely by an inability to differentiate between its two essential terms: self and image, subject and object. What is needed to mediate this dyad is language. In learning to speak the subject acquires names for itself and for the world outside it. It can make the essential distinctions required. However, this necessary gain involves a fundamental loss or alienation. The subject can name itself, but only at the expense of an irretrievable gap being opened up between the name and that which is named.

Lacan's point seems to be this: in using my name, be it the personal pronoun or family name, I employ a signifier. Now, given the 'primacy of the signifier', the sense of this personal signifier will be found only within the 'chain of the signifier'. My signified is, by definition, lost below the bar and, like all other signifieds, enjoys no local correspondence with its signifier. I am represented in language as 'I', and therefore excluded from language because replaced there by 'I'. This would seem to be the sense of Lacan's oft-repeated. 'The signifier is that which represents the subject for another signifier.'

Similarly, in naming the objects I want, I lose them as actual objects and have to do, instead, with their linguistic representatives or substitutes. In representing the world to the subject, and, through communication in a shared language, to others, words permit us to deal effectively with reality. Yet by standing for things, words stand between them and us. We gain the 'world' and lose the world.

One of Lacan's much favoured illustrations of this claim derives from Freud's famous *Fort! Da!* example. In *Beyond the Pleasure Principle*, Freud was concerned to understand instances of behaviour which apparently violated the postulated pleasure principle – that mental events are regulated, as far as is possible, by an avoidance of unpleasure and a production of pleasure. In the cases of 'traumatic neuroses', patients could be observed to dream of the original disaster or accident that occasioned the subsequent illness. Such evidence indicated an apparently inexplicable compulsion to repeat an unpleasant experience. In the same vein, Freud was led to make sense of one child's simple game.

This child, at 1½ years, developed a habit of making a cotton-reel disappear from his view, and, then, by means of the string attached to the reel, causing it to reappear. The disappearance was accompanied by an expressive 'ooh', and the return by a joyful '*da*' ('there'). Interpreting the 'ooh' as '*fort*' ('gone') led Freud to see the game as related to the disappearance and reappearance of his mother, to whom the child was greatly attached and who was in the habit of leaving the child for extended periods. But, given this perceived relation, how was one to understand the apparent repetition of an obviously distressing experience?

For Freud, the symbolization of the experience by the play with the reel, and alternation of the two sounds, enabled the child to master his situation. The child gained control of the mother's presence and absence by initiating, himself, the symbolic play that he made its substitute. Moreover, the child was able literally to become master. By making the mother disappear, the throwing away of the reel was a renunciation: from the passive, 'You're leaving me' to the active, 'I'm sending you away'.

This example serves Lacan's purpose of showing how, in language, the subject gains control over the real, but precisely by setting reality at a distance and interposing a sign. Of course, this characterization of language is, in many ways, rather unremarkable and certainly not original. It is, perhaps, no more than a sustained reflection upon the basic notion of the symbol, or word as standing for, and thus standing in for, i.e. replacing, the thing it denotes. But to go on to describe (as Lacan does) the sign as 'the murder of the thing' and as establishing 'presence against a background of absence, just as it constitutes absence in presence' is not only portentous, but misleading.

Moreover, Lacan would often appear to license an interpretation of his linguistic reading of Freud which sees it as no more than a linguistic reduction. The unconscious is simply that which is lost by the subject's entry into language; the bar in the Saussurean formula is to be taken literally as a barrier separating the subject of conscious discourse from his lost unconscious signification. 'Language is the condition of the unconscious' means here that language is the occasioning cause of the unconscious, and Lacan can interpret the embarrassing Freudian notion of the unconscious as primal by remarking that the primitivism of the unconscious means no more than the primacy of the signifier.

However, as was remarked earlier, Lacan offers not just a linguistic reading of Freud, but also a Freudian reading of language. Instead of simply substituting language acquisition for the primal repression which inaugurates the unconscious, Lacan gives the former a Freudian sense and context. This is accomplished by employing the notion of the Symbolic, which has wider connotations than simply language, and by introducing the Oedipal drama as the essential context for entrance into the Symbolic.

For all its importance and contentious significance in the history of psychoanalysis, Freud's notion of the Oedipus complex was never the subject of a single systematic account, and, indeed, underwent continuous revision in the course of his work. The child's first object of desire is the mother, and, of necessity, this implies a jealous hatred of his rival in this desire, the father. In turn, the child is threatened by the father, and feels this threat most directly in his fear of castration. The Oedipus complex first surfaces during that period, the phallic stage, in which the libidinal instincts are organized around the genitals. The initial failure to resolve the complex leads the child to suppress its sexuality and enter the so-called latency period. The complex resurfaces during puberty, where the extent to which, and manner in which, it is surmounted determines the individual's subsequent object-choice and orientation of desire. In its classical form, the complex is dissolved when the child displaces its desire from the forbidden object, the mother, on to similar but not identical objects, and internalizes the father's prohibition by identifying with this parent and thereby acquiring a super-ego.

Now there are celebrated difficulties with the theory of the Oedipus complex as formulated by Freud: the initial assumption of symmetry between male and female child, and the subsequent attempts to develop an asymmetrical and specific theory of female sexual development; the unclear location of the complex with respect to age and libidinal stages; the apparently culturally specific nature of the complex, demanding as it does the minimal family triad of father, mother and child. Lacan's adaptation of the Oedipal drama may be viewed, if not explicitly intended, as an attempt to resolve these problems by transposing all the dramatic elements to the level of the Symbolic.

In the Imaginary, the child desires. In terms borrowed from Hegel, the child desires the desire of the Other, in this instance the mother. Lacan fully exploits the ambiguity of the genitive to interpret this as meaning both that the child desires to be desired by the mother, and that the child desires that which is desired by the mother. The child thus identifies with the object of the mother's desire, the phallus. The phallus, in turn, is the imaginary completion of a perfect, merged union between child and mother, subject and Other. The Father forbids this union, and the child thereby encounters the Father's prohibition. The child surmounts the complex by identifying with the Father, and submitting to what the Father represents, namely the Law of the Symbolic. This, in turn, permits the child to internalize the prohibition on incestuous desire, acquire a status as a subject within the Symbolic, and see itself as one, like the Father, who has, rather than is, the phallus. The difference from Freud's account is that, for Lacan, the key terms in the drama are signifiers, not persons or fantasy figures. The phallus is not being identified with the biological organ, the penis, but rather thought of as the signifier of an original desire for a perfect union with the Other; the Father is not the real father, but, rather as Name-of-the-Father, signifier of the Law of the Symbolic. Employing a felicitous assonance, Lacan can identify the Name-of-the-Father (*nom-du-père*) with the Father's prohibition, his saying 'no' (*non-du-père*).

To complete this linguistic version of the Oedipal drama, Lacan provides a translation of the repression of the desire for the mother in terms of a metaphorical process. If we return to the Saussurean formula of the sign, metaphor can be represented as the substitution of one signifier for another to generate meaning. Lacan offers the following formalization of metaphor:

$$\frac{S}{S^1} \cdot \frac{\$^1}{x} \longrightarrow S\left(\frac{1}{s}\right)$$

The S's represent signifiers, S being the substitute for S^1, and x denotes an unknown signification, it being improper, on Lacan's account, to regard any individual signifier as having a fixed, correlate signified. It is the metaphoric substitution of one signifier for another which produces a meaning, and this is given by the presence of s below the bar on the right. A concrete example will illustrate what is being formalized:

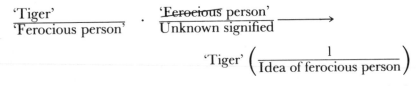

$$\frac{\text{'Tiger'}}{\text{'Ferocious person'}} \cdot \frac{\text{'\sout{Ferocious} person'}}{\text{Unknown signified}} \longrightarrow$$

$$\text{'Tiger'}\left(\frac{1}{\text{Idea of ferocious person}}\right)$$

The formula seems to have the formal correctness of a mathematical equation with the apparent multiplication of algebraic fractions. However, bearing in mind Lacan's fulminations against his disciples' later reading of the formula in just such a way, we should be cautious. Thus, the crossing out of S^1 should be taken only figuratively to indicate that, in the metaphoric process, 'tiger' comes to be the signifier united with the signified, ferocious person, by eliding or eliminating the intermediary signifier in the process, 'ferocious person'. Similarly, the figure '1' above the bar on the right can only presumably be intended to represent the stable registration of meaning by means of this single signifier.

If we move to the Oedipal drama, Lacan offers this formula for the paternal metaphor:

$$\frac{\text{Name-of-the-Father}}{\text{Desire of the Mother}} \cdot \frac{\text{Desire of the Mother}}{\text{Signified for the subject}} \longrightarrow$$

$$\text{Name-of-the-Father} \left(\frac{O}{\text{Phallus}} \right)$$

In the resolution of the Oedipal drama, the Name-of-the-Father substitutes for the desire of the mother, which represented an imaginary union of child and mother given by the phallus. This latter falls below the bar, and Lacan allows this to have the sense of being relegated beneath conscious discourse. What remains is the Symbolic order, whose law is represented by the Name-of-the-Father. The capitalized O, as an abbreviation of Other, is presumably intended to convey the sense whereby the desire originally signified by the phallus is, as a result of the metaphor, not stably registered by means of a single signifier but inscribed within the Other – that is, language, the chain of all signifiers.

None of this, least of all in Lacan's textual 'explication' of the formula, is clear and straightforward. One even has the uncomfortable feeling that we are being offered only a metaphor for the process of the paternal metaphor. Lacan does clearly assert that accession to the Symbolic is coincident with primal repression, that is, the institution of an unconscious; and that this is effected by means of a very particular metaphoric process. However, a number of crucial ambiguities assist his claim.

If it is objected that the use of metaphor is a function of an already acquired language, and that it is we, as language users, who construct metaphors, Lacan can respond that metaphor is an inherent feature of language, one of its fundamental axes. It thus determines our discourse in advance, as it were, of our speaking. Nevertheless, in depicting accession to language as a metaphoric process we are left with the uncomfortable question: Which comes first, language or metaphor? In the formula for the paternal metaphor, for instance, the phrase 'signified for the subject' is surely inappropriate designating as it does a pre-Symbolic, Imaginary, experience.

The problem cannot be posed unambiguously precisely because Lacan's use of the term, Symbolic, is unclear. He certainly intends it to have wider connotations than simply discourse or language.

71

Specifically, he borrows from Claude Lévi-Strauss the idea of a symbolic system, composed of language, laws, economic relations, art, science and religion, which structures human reality and pre-exists the conscious subject. The focal idea of the Symbolic is Law, and Lacan understands the symbolic Father, in his reading of the Oedipal drama, to represent this underpinning Law. This helps provide a response to the common charge against Freud's Oedipus complex: that it is a function of a very particular phenomenon, the bourgeois European family unit. On Lacan's interpretation, the culturally specific triad Father, Mother, Child, is replaced by a universal triad of Law, object and subject.

Moreover, understanding the Symbolic as both language and law might appear to deflect a common-sense observation that a child's acquisition of language significantly predates his or her initiation into the Oedipus complex. After all, the child of the *Fort! Da!* example, whom Lacan describes as at the point of insertion into the symbolic, is only 18 months old and some way off the moment of acceding to the Freudian, or Lacanian, father. If the Symbolic, whose legal agent the Father is, means more than just language, then the temporal disjunction is not so obviously an embarrassment to the theory.

However, things are slightly more complicated than that. There is a sense in which Lacan regards the Symbolic as, in Lévi-Strauss's terms, comprising more than just language. The Symbolic is the encoded, rule-governed institution of culture which, by means of its fundamental proscriptions – for instance, incest prohibitions or taboos – permits, and serves to define, human, as opposed to natural, existence. Now Lacan subscribes to the central tenet of 'structuralism': that the Saussurean method of inquiry into language can be extended so as to disclose and explain the structures of all human thought, behaviour and culture. For Lacan, the Symbolic is more than, but structured exactly like, language. Yet Lacan also, licenses the view that these rules of the Symbolic are written into language. So that, in acquiring the language we speak, we also, necessarily, acquire the rules by which we must, as humans, live. Lacan subsequently conflates the thesis that the Law of the Symbolic is distinct from, but homologous to, the law of all language and the contrary claim that the two are equivalent, that 'culture . . . could well be reduced to language or that which essentially distinguishes human society from natural societies'.[2]

Again, Lacan can argue that accession to language is a properly

72

Freudian process by his deployment of certain key elements of Freudian psychoanalysis – desire for the mother, phallus and father. How, though, are we to understand these terms? As signifiers in Lacan's usage of the word, 'Father' and 'phallus' have no necessary relation to any signifieds; they do not essentially refer to anything or have an established meaning. But, perhaps, on the contrary, Lacan intends the terms to be read as denoting what they would normally name. The former view is important, not least because insisting that the 'phallus' is distinct from the penis helps answer the charge that Freud ignores, or radically misrepresents, the specific nature of female sexuality. In talking about the phallus, Lacan's Freud is not referring to the biological organ which is the privileged possession of the male. We all have signifiers. In general terms, stressing that the Name-of-the-Father and phallus play their roles as signifiers is a crucial part of the linguistic reading of Freud.

Nevertheless, what gives that reading its Freudian conviction and force is precisely understanding castration anxiety as concern over a real object, and viewing the real father as he who is actually in a position to deprive the child of its mother's desire. In a sense, Lacan provides an Oedipal drama whose structure is more or less homologous to Freud's. He then claims that its elements are linguistic and not real entities. However, what makes the situation a drama of psychosexuality is surely that these elements are more than mere signifiers, and have a literal as well as metaphorical significance. The conflation of signifier in the sense of the simple sound or letters and as referring term permits some absurd rhetorical extravagances on the part of Lacan and his followers. Penises, as biological organs, may certainly have erections, but signifiers, as written or spoken words, most certainly do not.

For all its ambiguities, Lacan's account provides a striking response to the problem in Freud concerning the relation between the unconscious and repression. The problem can be expressed simply as: Which came first, the unconscious or repression? Freud defined repression as a mechanism of defence whereby something is turned away and kept at a distance from consciousness. It thus presupposes some kind of distinction between the unconscious and consciousness. Moreover, according to Freud, something cannot be repressed without two simultaneous influences acting upon it – attraction to the unconscious and repulsion from consciousness. This leaves us to understand how there is already an unconscious which can serve as the pole of attraction. Freud was forced to conclude that there is a 'primal' repression which institutes an original unconscious. Repression proper is then described as a kind of secondary repression which affects the derivatives, by associative connection, of that which was first laid down in the unconscious. This distinction has the appearance of a somewhat *ad hoc* adjustment to the theory and gives the unconscious something of a 'mythical' origin. Moreover, the posited distinction contrasts sharply with the view, expressed elsewhere by Freud, that everything was originally unconscious, and out of this, under the influence of the external world, consciousness subsequently developed.

Lacan's understanding of the distinction benefits from his promotion of language to the role of key Freudian motif. Primal repression is equated with accession to the Symbolic; the disjunction therein made between what the subject says and what is concealed by the very use of language corresponds to that between unconscious and conscious. Thereafter, the effects of the unconscious, in terms of the repressed and its return, the symptom, are comprehensible as the effects of language. It is here that Lacan's most celebrated dictum finds its place – 'the unconscious is structured like a language'. More specifically, Lacan assimilates the two processes of the Freudian unconscious, condensation and displacement, to the linguistic axes of metaphor and metonymy. Equally specific, but less clear, is Lacan's insistence that the symptom is a metaphor and desire a metonymy.

The phrase, 'structured like a language', is far less straightforward than its repeated use as an accessible resumé of Lacan's thought might suggest. In the first place, there is a distinction to be made between the effects or formations of the unconscious, and the unconcious itself. As was argued in Chapter 1, the distinction is by no means an easy one to make, since the conscious idea or behaviour from which the unconscious thought is inferred is the latter's disguised representation of itself to consciousness. It was suggested that Freud equivocates between regarding condensation and displacement as essential modes of unconscious mental activity, and as the effect of the censor's action upon the unconscious thought, whereby the latter secures disguised entry into consciousness. Lacan might similarly appear to be ambiguous between regarding metaphor and metonymy as somehow properties of an unconscious 'language', distinct from conscious discourse; and, on the other hand, as the effects of the unconscious upon conscious discourse. It is certainly the latter that Lacan intends, particularly when referring to the metaphor as a symptom, but then the celebrated dictum must be regarded as inexact.

In the second place, the use of structured 'like' or 'as' is ambiguous. When Lacan states that the laws of the unconscious are the same as those which create meaning in language, it is unclear whether he intends 'same' to mean exactly similar or strictly identical. In one sense, Lacan is only repeating his accord with the structuralists – the unconscious, like every other human phenomenon, exhibits a structure which can only be appreciated in terms of the kind of theory which Saussure applied to language. Unconscious and language are homologous but distinct. However, it is also the case that Lacan does seem to regard the unconscious as no more than the significatory opaqueness of language; the bar which separates signifier from signified is the barrier between consciousness and unconscious. Bearing all these ambiguities in mind would mean rendering Lacan's aphorism as: 'The unconscious, or rather its effects upon consciousness, are structured like, or indeed are possibly exactly equivalent to, the processes of language, namely metaphor and metonymy.'

Lacan's claim can be seen as an answer to Sartre's problem with the unconscious. In Chapter 2 we saw that Sartre understood the unconscious in terms of an occluded relationship between the symptom as signifier and the repressed desire as the signified which the former symbolically expressed. Sartre refused to understand this relationship of signification in terms of causality. He was thus forced to conclude that it was intra-subjectively constituted as one of comprehension. Sartre's problem then lay in explaining how such a relationship could both be constituted by, and be disguised from, one and the same consciousness. The thrust of Lacan's reply would be to deny the assumption, implicit in Sartre's account, that signification is to be found in a unique relationship between a particular signifier and its signified. Rather, as has been seen, in asserting the 'primacy of the signifier', Lacan repeatedly maintains that meaning 'insists' in the chain of all other signifiers, rather than consisting in one signifier's relation to its signified. Moreover, since the domain of the signifier is the Other, in the sense that language is public, unconscious meaning is a transubjective rather than, as with Sartre, narrowly intra-subjective phenomenon.

For Lacan, unconscious meaning 'insists' in the signifying chain by means of metaphor and metonymy. These Lacan equates with, respectively, condensation and displacement. Both the unconscious and the linguistic processes effect a translation by means of a substitution which involves an elision. The metaphoric shift from 'ferocious person' to 'tiger' in order to signify ferocious person elides the first signifier; the metonymic shift from 'I respect the person who wears the Crown' to 'I respect the Crown' in order to signify respect for the occupant of that office elides the signifier, 'the person who wears'. Following Jakobson, the metaphoric shift is accomplished by means of relations of similarity; and that of metonymy by an association of contiguity.

Let us apply the comparison between unconscious and linguistic processes to an example much favoured by Lacan and his critics: Freud's forgetting of the name, 'Signorelli'.[3] The example is immensely complicated and the diagram (Figure 1) is included as an illustrative aid. In the course of a journey Freud was discussing frescoes and could not remember the name of the painter Signorelli. While having a vivid image of this particular painter's face, Freud could only call to mind the names of two other painters, Botticelli and Boltraffio – both of which he knew to be incorrect. To anticipate the resolution of this forgetfulness, Freud discloses that the name 'Signorelli' was repressed because of its associations with the repressed topic of death and sexuality. Equally the substituted names, 'Botticelli' and 'Boltraffio', play their role because of their associations with this same topic.

To simplify the example here are some of the discovered associations:

1   *Signor*, the first element of the forgotten name, means the same as *Herr*. In describing the attitudes of Turks in Bosnia towards death and sexuality, a colleague of Freud had quoted his patients' remarks on these subjects which employed the opening form, '*Herr*(Sir) . . .'.

2   *Her(r)* in turn forms part of Herzegovina, conventionally associated with Bosnia.

3   The *Herz* of Herzegovina means 'heart', a 'sick bodily organ' suitable for symbolizing the repressed topic of death. Moreover, *Herz* (Hearts) is related as suit in the pack of cards to *Pick* (Spades), and this latter was the name of Freud's quoted authority on Bosnian attitudes towards the repressed topic.

Of the actually remembered names, 'Botticelli' comprises the 'Bo' of 'Bosnia', and the '-elli' of 'Signorelli'. 'Boltraffio' equally comprises 'Bo', and Freud discloses the '-traffio' to be linked to 'Trafoi', the name

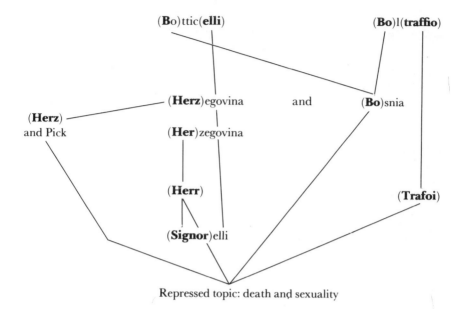

Figure 1   *The forgetting of 'Signorelli'*

of a place where news reached him of the suicide of one of his patients on account of 'an incurable sexual complaint'.

Now what can be said of this example as set forth? An unsympathetic critic of Freud might retort that the purported analysis is simply unbelievable, anything being provable with such elaborate and extended word play. Ironically, such an impression is strengthened when those sympathetic to Freud suggest further associations – the forgetting of Signorelli's first name, *Luca* (light), for instance, being related to Freud's first sighting of gas lighting on a significant train journey, or that 'Signorelli' begins with the same letters as Freud's own Christian name.

Nevertheless, if we suspend our disbelief, the example favours a Lacanian approach, principally because the associations are made at the level of the signifier. 'Signorelli' is significant as a name, not by designating the painter of particular works, but rather as one permitting certain associative word links. This is similarly true of 'Botticelli' and 'Boltraffio'. Curiously, we might object not that these

77

links are far fetched and convoluted, but that, in some cases compared with others, they are surprisingly direct. For instance, 'Signor' is transmuted into the 'Bo-' of both 'Botticelli' and 'Boltraffio' by means of an extended chain: Signor(elli)–Herr–Her(zegovina)–Bo(snia)–Bo(tticelli)/(ltraffio); whereas the 'elli' of 'Botticelli' is an undistorted reproduction of this element in the repressed word. Similarly, the '-traffio' of 'Boltraffio' reproduces, in a more or less straightforward manner, the name of a place directly associated with the repressed topic. We might wonder too why the associative links which forbid Signorelli entrance into consciousness equally permit the two substitutes to become conscious.

Further, the description of the associative links as metaphoric and metonymic leaves it unclear whether normal usage of these terms is being illegitimately extended or Jakobson's usage is being loosely applied. For example, metaphor is used to define a simple homophony (the 'Bo' of 'Bosnia' and 'Botticelli'/'Boltraffio'), a punning homophony ('Pick' as both a proper name and designating a suit of cards), or equivalence of meaning ('Signor' = 'Herr'). Metaphor comprises both similarity of sound and meaning. Metonymy may imply contiguity of syllables ('Her(z)' and 'egovina') or of words ('Herzegovina' and 'Bosnia').

Furthermore, it is not easy, in this example at least, to find simple equivalences between metaphor/metonymy and condensation/displacement. The actually remembered names, as symptomatic formations, may be regarded as metaphoric substitutes for the lost name – all three similarly designate painters. Moreover, the single word, 'Botticelli', by virtue of its separable elements and their associations, offers a condensed representation of a number of unconscious memories and thoughts. However, this condensation is not a simple metaphor, wherein a single signifier condenses two signifieds – its own and that of the elided, substituted signifier. The condensation described above is effected only by means of a series of both metonymic and metaphoric shifts that eventually link 'Botticelli' to 'Signorelli'. Again, the substitution of 'Botticelli'/'Boltraffio' for 'Signorelli' may also be described as a displacement from the significant painter's name on to the insignificant. Indeed, Freud describes the shift as a displacement. But, then, there is no simple equivalence with a metonymic process.

None of this is to deny that there are instances where a strict equivalence can be found; nor is it to deny that the notions of metaphor and metonymy, generously extended in meaning, can help our understanding of Freud's examples. What must be accepted is, first, that the processes of condensation and displacement do not receive from Freud clear and unambiguous definitions in their application to all psychoanalytic phenomena. Second, no strict equivalence between the two unconscious processes and their claimed linguistic correlates can be found in every single instance. Moreover, Lacan himself nowhere systematically applies his theoretical suggestion to a concrete example.

What remains outstanding from Freud's example is an explanation of its dynamics, namely the psychic energy deployed in repression and the formation of symptoms. From the economic point of view, condensation and displacement describe, respectively, a concentration of energies from different sources upon a single idea, and the detachment of energy from one idea and its free passage along associative pathways to other ideas. Chapter 1 considered the uneasy tension between the languages of psychic energy and of disguised symbolization. What account does Lacan offer of this aspect of Freudianism?

The key term in the account is Desire, but perhaps no other term in the Lacanian lexicon is so protean or resistant to clear definition. Several commentators have confessed their inability to elucidate its meaning, though its function seems clear. It libidinizes language and justifies Lacan's implicit claim to have supplemented a linguistic reading of Freud with a Freudian reading of language. What makes language the site of both the symptom and the possible cure is the fact that human desire is inscribed within the signifying chain and condemned to shift from one signifier to another. Desire, says Lacan, is a metonymy; or more specifically, desire is the metonymy of the want-to-be.

Let us spell out this claim. Desire is, in the first instance, distinct from need. A human individual has certain real biological needs which can be satisfied by specific objects: hunger and food, for instance. In the domain of the psychic no such simple relation obtains between lack and real object. For Freud, wishes were fulfilled by the hallucinatory reproduction of the perceptions associated with an earlier pleasurable experience. A wish can be fulfilled by dreaming of eating a meal in a way that the need, hunger, cannot.

To this fundamental distinction, Lacan adds the effect of the entry into language. As we have seen, language, by standing for objects, stands between the subject and objects. More specifically, if we accept

79

the role of the paternal metaphor, the subject is condemned to search in the realm of the signifier for the lost forbidden object: the imaginary union with the mother. It is at this level of the Symbolic that Lacan makes a distinction between Demand and Desire. The distinction is by no means clear, but seems to amount to this at least: demands, plural, are what the subject articulates in language; desire, singular, is the how and why of this articulation.

The human individual, in speaking, demands certain things. The demand is always addressed to another person. This is taken to imply both that one asks for something from the other, and that any demand is, in essence, a demand for love by the other. Demand, like desire, is distinct from need in that no object can satisfy it.

But why does the individual make such demands which essentially can never be satisfied? Because the individual is desire, and this desire is eternal, absolute and singular. How does the individual make such demands? By shifting from one object to another, in so far as an original desire finds its sense metonymically in the whole chain of signifiers. Lacan's human being desires something that has been lost, but the loss is irretrievable for the search must be conducted by means of that which forever separates the subject from the desired object: language. It is in this sense that Lacan suggests the object of desire to be its cause.

At this point too we should note Lacan's grafting of Hegel on to Freud. His repeated statement that 'man's desire is desire of the Other' owes much to Hegel, and in particular to the celebrated lectures by Kojève on Hegel which he, along with Sartre, Merleau-Ponty and others, attended. Kojève's pivotal interpretation of the Master–Slave dialectic from the *Phenomenology of Spirit* specified that human desire differs from mere animal desire in being a desire for recognition: the human being desires the desire of the Other. Lacan allows his use of this latter statement to have the sense Kojève gave it, but, once more making use of the genitive ambiguity, gives it another meaning. The human being desires *qua* Other, in that its desires are inscribed within the realm of the Other, language, and simultaneously desires as other than itself, namely unconsciously.

In describing desire as the metonymy of the want-to-be or lack of being, Lacan seems to give it a source in human nature. Ironically, Lacan is closest here to Sartre in defining the human being as both a lack of and desire for being. Unlike Sartre's fundamental ontology, Lacan's own notion of lack is an uneasy amalgam of the psychological, metaphysical and biological. At one level, the lack is straightforwardly defined as the loss of the imaginary union with the mother. Since this loss coincides with entry into the Symbolic, it is compounded. The individual can only try to find the meaning of its loss and recover it within the sphere of language. But language itself involves a loss of the object in general – and of the subject in so far as that which originally desired now finds itself only a signifier among other signifiers.

In places, however, Lacan hints that the original striving for a complementing union with the mother is an index of a more fundamental lack of being on the part of the human subject. Either this is an unexplained ontological postulate or ambiguously related to biological fact. In the simplest sense, birth itself is a loss on the child's part of union with the mother. It is separated from that which previously formed its anatomical complement. In a slightly different vein, Lacan, in the 'mirror-stage' article, refers to the specific prematurity of birth in the human. By this he means that the child is born in advance of a completed neurological development. It is, in part, this sensed lack of a complete self whch precipitates the child into a motivated misrecognition of itself as the co-ordinated, matured and complete mirror image.

The problem with all this is that it simply takes for granted a certain biological grounding for human desire without any satisfactory explanation of how the physiological is translated into the psychological, how the individual experiences at the level of Desire that which originates at a completely different level. Lacan might well reply that desire is that which is to be explained, rather than that which serves as an ultimate explanatory notion. Moreover, the ultimate meaning of an individual's life lies in a stage that predates and underpins both the imaginary and symbolic. As such, it is, as far as Lacan is concerned, unthinkable. The most we can do is go in search of a source which we are condemned to meet only in its derivative effects. Lacan was certainly disposed to caution against a cognitive totalitarianism which wanted to know all, and remained dissatisfied with stopping at the barriers of the unknown. We should learn to recognize that human truth is of a different order, and at a permanent remove, from knowledge, thought and language.

But then it must be said that we are left with a speculative notion of original experiences. Moreover, we are far from Freud's own careful work on a theory of instincts which tried to prepare psychoanalysis for its eventual reconciliation with biology and physiology. To promote desire to the role of central psychoanalytic concept and insist upon its specifically psychical sense is a legitimate move if it is believed that psychoanalysis can only thus be salvaged from the encroachments of a vulgar biological materialism. However, Freud's own separation of the domains of psychology and physiology, whatever its occasional ambiguities, was intended, for methodological reasons, only to postpone their eventual reconciliation, not to effect an ontological dualism. In this respect, Lacan's use of a Hegelian notion of desire, and his concept of an irreducible human lack, instead of a more orthodox Freudian theory of instincts, is significant. Lacan is more of a speculative thinker the further he moves away from Freud.

There is a further problem with the notion of desire disclosed by the indefinite article in Lacan's definition of desire as a metonymy. Metonymy is regarded by Lacan as a fundamental axis, or inherent feature, of language. On the one hand, it might seem that this axis is simply identical with human desire. The individual desires in so far as, and just to the extent that, s/he speaks metonymically. But the metonymies are specified in advance of, and outside the control of, the individual by a pre-existing structure. This would certainly make desire the property of the Other, language, but would entail denying any notion of specifically individual motivations. It is an impersonal unconscious which, Lacan likes to claim, 'speaks' in language.

On the other hand, if individual desires make use of language, we are in need of some account of the particular motivated articulation of desire that characterizes each human being. There is no doubt, for instance, that a forgetting like that of 'Signorelli' is inexplicable without reference to the special history of the individual who forgets. In linguistic terms, Lacan's notion of desire lies uneasily suspended between being a mere aspect of the Code, and functioning within individual Messages. Emphasizing the former yields an abstract, impersonal Desire which is common to all human beings and specific to none; stressing the latter demands some account of intentionality or motivation.

In defining the unconscious as the discourse of the Other, the polysemy of the key term, Other, serves to condense Lacan's central claims. The site of the unconscious is the alienated realm of language; the unconscious is radically heterogeneous and ex-centric to the place where the subject thinks it knows itself to be itself; the Other is the object and cause of that desire which traverses our speech, and is lost therein. The unconscious, for Lacan, means that the subject speaks in

82

the place of the Other, as Other, and of the Other. In the last analysis, the failure adequately to specify the concept of desire means that what is left in suspense is the fundamental motor of the unconsious – the nature of that which, at source, speaks and the why it has to speak.

The Lacanian account of the unconscious suffers from the fact that the Freudian reading of language is not adequate to the linguistic reading of Freud. Lacan's Freud is a hermeneutist of the unconscious text, whose subtle and complex associations would seem to require prodigious interpretative skills. This reading of Freud rests upon a peculiarly Lacanian understanding, or misunderstanding, of linguistics. Yet Freudian energetics receive little, if any, attention. Lacan either refuses to offer an account of what is meant by instinctual energy, or opts instead for speculative theory.

This is not a pardonable omission. As was argued in Chapter 1, hermeneutics and energetics do not simply represent alternative and, for some, incompatible, explanatory languages. They derive their respective plausibilities, and ultimately their comprehensibility, from two incompatible theories of mind – a dualist and a monist or reductionist one. Unfortunately, a large number of Freudian critics appear to accept as self-evident that 'reductionist' or 'vulgar' biological materialism is incompatible with psychoanalysis properly understood. But, if a dualist account of Freud is being offered (and the 'for the present' of Freud's celebrated phrase has enjoyed a seemingly ever prolonged duration), then serious effort must be made to explain how desire, energy, pleasure, libido, instincts make sense at the purely psychical level. If we are being asked to accept parallelism, then biological evidence of whatever kind is simply beside the point. If it is an interactionist version of dualism which is being presented, then defenders of Freud, and Lacan, must answer that most basic criticism of all such accounts: how does the irreducibly psychical interact with the irreducibly physiological. The claim that the unconscious is the domain of the instinctual 'representative', not the somatic instinct, is simply an evasion of the point at issue, and, without further explanation, incomprehensible. Freud's biological grounding of the unconscious in the sexual instincts offered some account of its mental dynamics. To accept, or assume, such a base and yet, without offering any reasoned alternative, repudiate 'vulgar reductionism', is to render unintelligible the whole notion of the psychic.

And Lacan's psychic is ineffable. This chapter has conceded Lacan a 'voice' which, even by the cautiously expressed sentiments of its opening pages, cannot formulate an argument to be assessed and criticized. If the 'primacy of the signifier' is taken seriously, then, even apart from its arguable incoherence as a theory of meaning, its significance is to make of Lacan's work an untranslatable, rhetorical text. On Lacan's terms, dismissal of a second-hand, synoptic rendering of his work is perfectly comprehensible and licit. But then his readers, with or without the benefit of such an attempted guide, are equally at liberty to reject the original as making no, or palpably bad, sense.

Notes

1 'The agency of the letter in the unconscious or reason since Freud', in, *Écrits, A Selection* (translated by Alan Sheridan; London 1977), p. 153.
2 ibid., p. 148.
3 The example can be found in 'The psychical mechanism of forgetfulness', *SE*, III, pp. 289–97; and 'The psychopathology of everyday life', *SE*, VI, especially pp. 2–7.

Further reading

Lacan's most celebrated text, the *Écrits*, originally published by Éditions du Seuil in 1966, has received a partial English translation as *Écrits, A Selection* (translated by Alan Sheridan; London 1977). A key piece from the *Écrits*, 'The function and field of speech and language in psychoanalysis', appeared in an earlier translation, *The Language of the Self* (London 1968). The translator, Anthony Wilden, also provides extensive explanatory notes, as well as a lengthy essay of critical exposition, 'Lacan and the discourse of the Other'. This latter has all the merits and defects of extremely close attention to the original.

Transcripts of Lacan's seminars, a volume for each year, are being published in France. So far only a single volume of these has been translated: Jacques-Alain Miller (ed.), *The Four Fundamental Concepts of Psycho-Analysis* (translated by Alan Sheridan; London 1979).

Discussions of some of the specific themes considered in this chapter can be found in the following articles from the translation of *Écrits*:

Saussurean linguistics and the 'primacy of the signifier', in 'Agency of the letter of the unconscious'; the mirror-stage and the Imaginary, in 'The mirror stage'; the 'paternal metaphor' and the Oedipus complex, in 'On the possible treatment of psychosis', especially section 4; desire and demand, in 'Direction of treatment and principles of its power', especially section 5.

Of the secondary critical texts, Anika Lemaire's *Jacques Lacan* (translated by David Macey; London 1977), is a commendably systematic, ordered and clear presentation. Richard Wollheim's review article, 'The Cabinet of Dr. Lacan', *New York Review of Books*, **25** nos. 21–2 (January 1979), pp. 36–45, has the merit of treating Lacan seriously, but by no means uncritically, and its author's familiarity with Freud informs writing of commendable rigour and clarity. J. Laplanche and J. B. Pontalis, *The Language of Psycho-Analysis* (London 1980), remains an invaluable guide to the key Lacanian concepts.

Ferdinand de Saussure's science of linguistics can be found in his *Course in General Linguistics* (Glasgow 1974) and admirably summarized in Jonathan Culler's *Saussure* (Glasgow 1976). The ideas of Roman Jakobson especially relevant to Lacan and this chapter may be found in Part II of Jakobson and Morris Halle, *Fundamentals of Linguistics* (The Hague/Paris 1971).

For a lucid and stimulating introduction to the treatment within Anglo-American philosophy of the problems of language and meaning, see Ian Hacking's *Why does language matter to philosophy?* (Cambridge 1976).

4

The unconscious as language

In October–November 1960 a colloquium on the subject of the unconscious was held in Bonneval, France, and attended by both psychoanalysts and philosophers. Lacan himself delivered a paper, but the event will probably be remembered chiefly for a contribution from two of his pupils, Jean Laplanche and Serge Leclaire. Their paper, 'The Unconscious: a psychoanalytic study', originally appeared in *Les Temps modernes*, and has since received an English translation.

In this form, it has offered English readers an accessible, lucid and apparently faithful account of Lacan's ideas about the unconscious and language. It was therefore dismaying for these same readers to hear subsequently of Lacan's own passionate disavowal of his former pupils' work. The disavowal was so bitter as to remind one of Freud's contempt for those who misunderstood his original and founding work. Moreover, the tenor of Lacan's rejection was so little compatible with the accepted rules of academic discussion that even a French critic sympathetic to Lacan felt it severely prejudiced that author's original claims.[1]

Nevertheless, because of, rather than despite, this impassioned repudiation, Laplanche's and Leclaire's contribution has an exemplary value in helping one to understand Lacan's reading of Freud. It has the merit of seeking to elucidate clearly a set of problems inherent in this reading. Lacan may well feel that its proposed resolution of these problems does his own work an extreme disservice. However, such a misunderstanding is at least a motivated one, and comes from authors who cannot easily be dismissed as unsympathetic or ill-informed.

Laplanche's and Leclaire's text is a 'dated' one, and, without the dubious benefit of Lacan's personal *auto-da-fé*, would probably have little contemporary interest. Other subsequent work by Leclaire, in particular, might be thought of more significance. Nevertheless, it has had a vast influence in the English-speaking world, where, first, it has been explicitly employed as a shorthand guide to Lacan's principal views on the unconscious; second, and this perhaps explains this influence, it does seek to render Lacan's account of the Freudian unconscious in a coherent and intelligible fashion, and thus, perhaps unwittingly, illuminates its failings; and third, it explicitly contrasts the 'properly Freudian' notion of the unconscious with the Politzerian and Sartrean 'bowdlerizations' of it. It should be added that though the article is conventionally cited under a dual signature, it does in fact comprise two distinct, if interrelated, contributions – that from Laplanche being the most substantial and, for Lacan, most culpably heterodox.

Laplanche commences his account with a response to Politzer, who, as seen in Chapter 2, accused Freud of an unwarranted 'realism' about the unconscious. For Politzer, the distinction between manifest and latent content of a dream did not justify speaking of two distinct and equally real psychological entities or agencies, the unconscious and consciousness. The relation between the two contents is simply one of meaning; the reported dream is the direct expression, albeit in unconventional terms, of the wish. One should not, as Freud unfortunately did, seek to locate the 'wish' and 'dream report' in two separate mental realms.

In response, Laplanche insists upon the radical heterogeneity of conscious and unconscious. Freud drew attention to the evidence provided by both normal and pathological phenomena of a conflict between, or convergence of, two distinguishable sets of forces or processes. Thus, for instance, slips of the tongue make sense as the mutual interference between two different intended remarks; dreams may be understood as compromise formations which secure the fulfilment of an unconscious wish under the disguise imposed by a censor. Notions of conflict, interference, compromise, make no sense if the unconscious is treated, in Politzer's way, as merely the meaning immanent to the conscious phenomenon. A meaning cannot sensibly be said to interfere or conflict with the sign which expresses it.

Furthermore, Laplanche understands Freud's 1915 metapsychological paper, 'The Unconscious', as being entirely concerned with a search for the basis of this real distinction between the two realms. Laplanche is astute enough to recognize, and make precise, a hesitation on Freud's part between two alternative explanations of this systematic distinction. One particular problem, that of the so-called 'double inscription', serves as a means of choosing between the two competing explanations.

The topographical hypothesis conceives of the unconscious and consciousness as two places or sites in the mind. A consequence of this view is that when an idea is transposed from one system into another, a second registration or inscription of the idea in question should be effected. Two registrations of the same idea coexist in the psychic apparatus, but in each of its two different psychic parts. The functional hypothesis, on the other hand, defines the distinction between the two systems from the economic point of view, that is, in terms of the psychic energy specific to each system. From such a viewpoint, the transposition of an idea from one system to another consists only in a change of its state, that is, the quantifiable energy with which it is cathected. The presence of an idea in one system entails its absence from the other.

The thesis of 'double inscription' would appear to be confirmed by at least one notable fact of analytic practice. A patient may be informed of an idea which the analyst knows to have been repressed at some previous stage. However, the communication does not in any way alter the mental condition resultant from this original repression. Such a change might be expected to follow from an unconscious idea becoming conscious. So it would appear that the analysand possesses two inscriptions of the same idea in different psychic locations – the repressed unconscious memory and the conscious auditory impression of the communicated idea. The patient can hear, and have a conscious idea of, for instance, 'the father's death', and yet still retain a repressed, unconscious memory of this same 'father's death'. Freud does not, however, immediately accept that such evidence confirms the thesis of 'double inscription' – nothing conclusively establishes that it is exactly the same idea which is inscribed in two places.

Indeed, such problems provoke Freud into a more systematic elaboration of what he means by 'idea'. We are concerned here with what, crudely, can be said to be 'in' the unconscious and consciousness. In the first instance, it is necessary to distinguish between the instinct or drive which is biological in origin and character, and its so-called 'representative' which is properly psychical. Only the latter can be found in the unconscious or consciousness. Freud further defines the instinctual representative as an idea which is charged, or 'cathected', with a definite quota of psychic energy, or 'affect'. Each of these two elements undergoes a different fate in the process of repression and, consequently, the constitution of the unconscious.

Briefly, the primal repression which inaugurates the unconscious involves the ideational representative of an instinct being excluded from consciousness. There is thereby established a 'fixation'. Crudely, the representative is stuck in the unconscious, and the instinct remains stuck to its representative. Subsequent repression involves ideas being pushed out of consciousness, and simultaneously dragged into the unconscious by virtue of their association with these first representatives. The 'Signorelli' example, discussed in Chapter 3, explained the fate of this particular word by virtue of its relationship to the repressed themes of death and sexuality. Equally, it is the derivatives of the originally repressed representatives which seek entry into consciousness. They succeed in proportion to their associative distance from, or degree of distortion of, the repressed representative. Again, the replacement of 'Signorelli' by 'Botticelli' and 'Boltraffio' in the cited example bears witness to this claim.

While the ideational representative is thus fixxed, the quota of affect can become detached from the idea and undergo a variety of fates, according to whether it is suppressed or finds expression in consciously experienced affect, such as anxiety. Freud is quite clear and specific that, in examining repression, it is necessary to explore both the different fates of an idea and the psychic energy originally linked to it. Nevertheless, he regards it as proper only to speak of ideas as contained within the unconscious. They are actually inscribed or registered within that psychic system. Affects, on the other hand, are only processes of discharge and not accurately described as 'unconscious'.

Thus far, Freud's account favours the topographical hypothesis with its implication of a double inscription of the same ideas. However, in the final section of his 1915 paper, Freud makes a further distinction within the ideational representative between the essentially auditory presentation of the word and the essentially visual presentation of the thing. This distinction, mentioned briefly in Chapter 1, provides him with a criterion whereby conscious and unconscious ideas may be distinguished. The conscious idea comprises both the presentation of the thing, and that of the word belonging to it. The unconscious idea is solely the presentation of the thing, becoming preconscious by connecting with the word-presentation corresponding to it. This means both that the preconscious is intimately connected with the linguistic function, and that repression amounts to an idea not being verbalized or put into words.

Freud's conception of an idea as a dual presentation would appear to resolve his indecision over the basis of the distinction between the unconscious and consciousness. A simple topographical thesis in terms of the double inscription of the same idea cannot be accepted, since unconscious and conscious ideas are not, as Freud initially suspected, the same. Equally, the difference cannot be accounted for, as the functional hypothesis would have it, by a simple change in psychic energy. It is the ideas themselves that change between the unconscious and conscious systems.

Laplanche's central claim would appear to be that these Freudian insights can properly be elucidated by translating them directly into the terms of the Lacanian schema. One then has an adequate account of what is meant by repression, what is in the unconscious, and lastly, how the unconscious is related to the preconscious/conscious. Before assessing the success of this translation it is necessary to set out Laplanche's thesis. For Laplanche, it is proper to speak of a mythical stage preceding the institution of the unconscious, wherein the individual utilizes a primitive and much reduced language. Primal repression effects a separation between the unconscious and preconscious/conscious. The unconscious is constituted as a chain of 'key signifiers' which both fix the previously unbound instinctual energy and, more crucially, anchor preconscious language by ensuring relatively stable relationship of signifier to signified.

At the centre of Laplanche's argument is his employment of Lacan's formula for the metaphor. This was considered in Chapter 3 and could be formalized as:

$$\frac{S^1}{S} \times \frac{S}{s} \longrightarrow S^1 \times \frac{1}{s}$$

Interpreting the above as a strict algebraic formula, Laplanche writes it as:

$$\frac{S^1}{S} \times \frac{S}{s} \longrightarrow \frac{\dfrac{S^1}{s}}{\dfrac{S}{S}}$$

and maintains that this formula is an exact representation of repression.

Moreover, it yields a formalization of both the unconscious below the main bar on the right, namely $\frac{S}{S}$, and of the preconscious/conscious above the bar, $\frac{S^1}{s}$. Laplanche argues that the formula adequately represents both primal repression and repression proper. The latter, as we have seen, consists of an idea being attracted into the unconscious by elements already existing there, and replaced simultaneously in consciousness by an associated derivative. This seems to accord more or less with the formalized process of metaphor. One signifier, S^1, replaces another, S, which consequently falls below the bar. It is the association of the replaced signifiers with signifiers already present below the bar which is essential to the process.

Leclaire's contribution to the article consists of the presentation and analysis of a specimen dream from one of his patients, Philippe. An example drawn from this analysis will serve to illustrate the process. The presence in the reported dream of the word *place* (scene) is argued to be the substitute for repressed memories associated with a beach, *plage*. The phonetic similarity of *place* and *plage* allows us to speak of a metaphoric substitution, so that, in terms of the formula, we have:

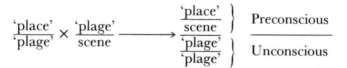

To complete the illustration we should note that, for Leclaire, the repressed term *plage*, is able to connect with elements already present in the unconscious. In the case of Philippe, a key signifier in the unconscious is 'je'. The homophony of 'je' and the '-ge' of 'plage' is what permits the necessary connection. We will return to the mysterious duplication of signifiers below the bar.

If the formula represents repression itself, what of the primal repression which is supposed to institute the unconscious in the first place? Laplanche argues the necessity of positing a certain mythical state before the separation of unconscious and consciousness. He ascribes to this stage the fiction of language in a reduced state. It is language in so far as it is characterizable in terms of the Saussurean formula for the sign. What is minimally required for a signifier to signify is that it be distinguishable from, or opposed to, another signifier.

Laplanche's citation, in this respect, of the *Fort! Da!* example is worth quoting:

If, by allowing him to master them, the opposite pair of phonemes A–O come to symbolise for the child the presence and absence of his mother, is it not by this same movement that presence and absence are themselves constituted as the two categories into which the child's whole universe is divided, whereas previously . . . it was wholly and without mediation satiety or void.[2]

This, concludes Laplanche, is akin to the myth of Genesis wherein, 'in a single motion, the separation and naming of heaven and earth occur'. As quoted, Laplanche's argument is fallacious. The child was already able to make certain distinctions, namely mother/father, child/mother, child/father. Thus the child comprehended distinctions in what was not a homogeneous and undivided universe, and, crucially, did not have signifiers to mark, or, on Laplanche's apparently stronger claim, to simultaneously effect these distinctions. The conclusion that any such distinctions are coextensive with and contemporaneous with the use of differentiated signifiers cannot be sustained.

However, Laplanche wants to use his example in one specific way, namely to reinforce Lacan's doctrine of the 'primacy of the signifier'. In the reduced case there are four terms, two signifiers ('O' and 'A'), and two signifieds (the ideas of absence and presence). Each signifier, it is being claimed, can play its signifying role only by virtue of its differential relation to all other signifiers. In the reduced case, this means a relationship between only two signifiers. The O–A phonetic opposition or difference can signify the opposition, 'absence'/'presence', but there is no 'natural' or 'motivated' relationship between either one of the signifiers and either of their corresponding signifieds.

Laplanche extends the argument to claim that such a phonetic opposition could be used to signify other significant oppositions in the individual's universe. Laplanche suggests that in this primitive language just such a sliding of opposed signifiers across the signified does occur. The language of schizophrenics supposedly provides a glimpse of this possibility, wherein, for instance, the pair 'right'/'left' is used to signify a whole series of opposed meanings: 'right' meaning 'the maladjusted' as well as 'getting along with my family'. Laplanche's thesis of the reduced language would appear to be a radical version of the Lacanian 'sliding' of the signifier over the signified, in conjunction with a posited minimal set of signifying pairs.

However, as it stands, this thesis is incoherent. It is claimed that a speaker's use of the same word, for example, 'right', can convey different meanings, for example, of spatial location, mental state, relation to family. Either the speaker does or does not comprehend these different senses of 'right'. If s/he does then there will be means of indicating them by accompanying gestures, clarificatory synonyms, or, however, such that the speaker can show s/he means 'right' in the sense of 'on my right-hand side' as opposed to 'insane'. In this case it is oversimplifying things to claim that the pair 'right'/'left' covers different oppositions of meaning. Rather, in different and distinguishable contexts. the same words can mean different things. If the speaker does not comprehend these different senses, then clearly it is not the case that the pair 'right'/'left' covers 'a whole series of opposed meanings'. Or rather, this speaker's use of 'right'/'left' covers what *for us* may be a whole series of opposed meanings, but between which s/he is unable to make' any conceptual distinction.

Laplanche continues by suggesting that preconscious language use, in contradistinction to the 'primitive language', is relatively stable with meanings fixed at certain points of the signifying chain. It is primal repression which arrests the radical sliding evident in the reduced language. It does so by fixing certain 'key signifiers' in the unconscious, their metaphorical substitutes in consciousness thus having a certain anchorage or ballast. There are privileged points at which the slide of the signifier over the signified, characterizing conscious discourse, is arrested because the preconscious/conscious signifier has a metaphorical relation to a signifier down below the bar in the unconscious. Borrowing a term of Lacan's, Laplanche refers to these as *points de capiton* – literally the buttons which hold upholstery down. These key signifiers also serve to fix the instinctual drive in the unconcious, as did Freud's original ideational representatives. In his analysis of Philippe's dream, Leclaire demonstrates how a set of key signifiers, *J'ai soif*, fix his otherwise undifferentiated instinctual energy, order his entry into language and provide the basis of explanations for the subsequent repressions and symptomatic behaviours, namely the metaphoric substitution of 'place' for 'plage'.

It would seem, then, that for Laplanche and Leclaire, the unconscious consists of signifiers, initially the key and anchoring signifiers, subsequently those attracted by associative connections into the initial chain. Yet, on the one hand, the formula yields $\frac{S}{S}$ as a representation of the unconscious element; on the other, Laplanche claims to be faithful to Freud who, as we have seen, specifically argued that only thing-presentations were present within the unconscious. Freud's distinction between word- and thing-presentation permits a certain comparison with the Saussurean distinction between signifier and signified, which would imply that it is not signifiers, only signifieds, that are to be found in the unconscious. Laplanche's response is simple enough in form. Both word- and thing-presentations should be understood as signifiers. The unconscious does indeed consist only of thing-presentations or 'images'. Although these images serve 'simultaneously and inseparably as signifier and signified', the unconscious chain is 'pure signifier' since it is 'open to all meanings'.[3] The formula $\frac{S}{S}$ is said to capture this claim perfectly.

Now there are a number of extraordinary confusions and ambiguities in Laplanche's account. He regards his understanding of the unconscious as according with Freud's view of this psychic system as governed by the primary process. Some comments of Freud license the view that this process has a certain curious 'language'. For instance, Freud remarks that, in schizophrenia, words are subject to the same process, the primary process, as that which constructs dreams – namely words are treated as though they were things, and meanings shift anarchically between words. Those who cite these comments ignore Freud's subsequent correction: the essential difference between schizophrenia and dreams is that, while in the former words are subject to the primary process, in the latter it is only thing-presentations that are so subject.[4] It would seem that Freud retains his conviction that the unconscious does not contain a 'language', only a string of thing-presentations cut off from the words that belong to them and which are essentially a function of the preconscious.

Laplanche tries to have it both ways. On the one hand, he claims that the unconscious is composed of signifiers because thing-presentations, which Freud said composed the unconscious, must be understood as elements of language, signifiers. On the other hand, these thing-presentations are merely images to which the distinction between signifier and signified does not apply, or rather, the signifying image refers to nothing but itself as signified. Again, if one refers back to the

94

formula for repression it is clear that what occurs in repression proper is that a signifier, in the normal usage of the term, is drawn below the bar by virtue of its associative connection with an already existing chain of signifiers. But how can a signifier, which is properly a signifier, contract associative connections with a chain of signifiers which are *not* properly signifiers? Certainly, one possible reading of the article, which emphasized Leclaire's contribution, would be that the unconscious chain does consist of signifiers, that is, words or phonetic elements, as, for example, the 'J'ai soif' in the case of Philippe. However, this cannot accord with Laplanche's professedly Freudian contention that the unconscious 'language' is merely a string of images.

Moreover, the key signifiers of the unconscious are said by Laplanche to play an anchoring role for the preconscious signifiers. The former prevent the latter from 'sliding' so much as to make any stable meaning impossible. Presumably, this occurs because the unconscious signifiers are univocal, and this permits their preconscious metaphorical substitutes to have, albeit at a certain remove, a fixity of meaning. But the key signifiers, by Laplanchean definition, are univocal in a trivial sense. Being both signifier and signified, they can only connote themselves and nothing else. A more pregnant sense of 'anchorage' would require that they be signifiers in another, that is, normal usage.

Laplanche is also loose in his use of the term 'primary process'. Both the mythic preconscious stage of reduced language, and the actual 'language' of the unconscious are said to be governed by the primary process, in so far as both are characterized by a certain evanescence or instability of meaning. Yet he is honest enough to admit a difference between the two. The mythic first language of bare differential pairs does at least operate by means of a distinction between a signifier and a signified, which does not apply to the unconscious 'language' of images. Laplanche claims, however, that what 'slides' in the latter is not the signifier over the signified, but pure psychic energy. This is unsatisfactory. The free mobility of energy characteristic of the unconscious or primary processes is not simply equivalent to the 'dizziness' of meaning imputed to unconscious ideas. Moreover, it is precisely an account of the unbound energy of the unconscious which is absent from Laplanche's exposition.

In the earlier section of the article, Laplanche describes the economic hypothesis as the most satisfactory explanation of the radical distinction between the unconscious and conscious systems, yet admits that it is difficult to give a precise meaning to the notion of a specific systemic energy. Pure psychic energy can only be specified as pertaining to one or other of the systems because it is attached to the ideational representative of either system. However, this would make the economic thesis depend upon an already established topographical separation of realms to which ideas respectively belonged.

Laplanche prefers to think of the cathectic energy specific to each system as a *Gestalt* within which individual elements assume their particular significance. The example he adopts is that of puzzle drawings, wherein, for instance, animals are discovered among the leaves of trees. The perceptual 'shift' from seeing just leaves to seeing animals is the equivalent of the shift from one system to another; the *Gestalt* of systemic energy is what maintains the leaves/animals in their relationship to the rest of the surrounding drawing. The example raises more problems that it claims to resolve. It appears to reduce systemic energy to the interrelationship between *ideas*, and it is perhaps significant that, in the quote from Freud's article on 'Repression' which Laplanche uses at this stage of his argument, Freud is referring to the *ideational* representatives of the instinct. Moreover, in considering energy only at the level of the system, Laplanche is forced to ignore Freud's own stipulations. It will be remembered that Freud described repression in terms of the two elements of any particular instinctual representative, the ideational representative and the quota of affect, and insisted that the vicissitudes they underwent were distinct. Indeed, he concluded that 'the vicissitude of the quota of affect belonging to the representative is far more important than the vicissitude of the idea, and this fact is decisive for our assessment of the process of repression'.[5] Laplanche's conception of systemic energy permits no such account to be taken of this quota of affect, and, in fact, it would seem that throughout his exposition what he means by the instinctual representative is merely the ideational representative.

Like Lacan, Laplanche tends to neglect the notion of psychic energy which is so important as a driving force within Freud's model of the psychic apparatus. Mobility of energy is simply displaced on to, and conflated with, the instability of meaning, and this latter is explained solely in terms of the components of the idea, signifier and signified, word- and thing-presentation. Metaphor, metonymy, shifts of meaning are invested with a dynamic that is left without a proper foundation. Yet again, the sophisticated hermeneutics of the

Freudian theory are preserved, and emphasized, at the expense of its energetics.

Lacan's own response to the Laplanche and Leclaire article is instructive. If one can ignore their rhetorical extravagances, his comments contain some substantive and illuminating points. In the first instance, Lacan objects strongly to the literal, that is mathematical, reading of the formula for metaphor which Laplanche places at the centre of his argument. Nothing, Lacan would claim, authorizes Laplanche's treatment of the Saussurean formula for the sign as an algebraic fraction; his subsequent multiplication and simplification of these fractions is thus completely unwarranted. Anticipating such an objection, the previous chapter offered an idiomatic interpretation of this formula and Lacan's use thereof. Laplanche's error is to have taken Lacan too 'seriously', though it is fair to comment that the latter's use of illustrative devices is ambiguous. It is, of course, perfectly legitimate to maintain that Lacan's formulae, schemes and graphs are merely 'good to think with', and that we will not go wrong if, following Freud's own prescription, we do not mistake the scaffolding for the building. However, one problem of interpreting Lacan is that it is not always so easy to discern the building behind the scaffolding. Laplanche's heresy is at least understandable, if not in Lacan's view excusable.

A further error of interpretation by Laplanche is his reading of the concept of the *points de capiton*. Laplanche employs the concept to explain the relative stability of preconscious language in terms of anchored unconscious signifiers. There are points at which, in the last instance, the signifier hooks on to a signified. Lacan understands the notion of *points de capiton* in a much less clear and straightforward manner. He speaks of a 'diachronic' function of the anchoring point within a sentence, whereby a term is anticipated by those that precede it, and, in turn, finally fixes the meaning of those others by its retroactive effect. The point would seem to be as follows. In a sentence, as it is uttered, the words to come can to some extent be anticipated on the basis of what has already been said. Equally, each word uttered only makes complete sense when the sentence is finished and it is perhaps only the very last word uttered which retrospectively establishes the full sense of each word that came before.

Let us take a simple example and see how much is established. As we hear the uncompleted sentence, 'The plane is . . .', we anticipate what is to come, knowing both that the sentence can be completed in a number

97

of possible ways, and that these various possibilities will differently fix the meaning of what we have already heard. For instance, this sentence might be completed in one of the following ways: 'an invaluable tool for any carpenter'; 'bound for New York'; 'a tree with fan-shaped leaves'; or 'an important geometrical concept'. Now it is true that we recognize the sense of the word, 'plane', only when the sentence has been completed. True also that the information given by the sentence differs according to what sense the word has. However, the range of possible understandings is limited and the context in which the sentence occurs will make one or some more probable than the others. Moreover, these different senses of the word can clearly be distinguished from one another by definitions or synonyms. It is difficult to see how the 'diachronic anchoring point' stops anything but the most minimal sliding of signifier over signified.

Lacan also alludes to a 'synchronic' aspect of the anchoring point. He appears to be referring to a notional origin or source of meaning, whereby signifiers are fixed to signifieds. Now this takes us to the very heart of Lacan's theory of language, and his (mis)interpretation of Saussure. As we saw in Chapter 3, Lacan understands Saussure's doctrine of the arbitrariness of the sign to entail the lack of any necessary relationship between a signifier and a signified. Consequently, each signifier can only be understood in terms of its relation to all other signifiers, rather than to any signified. But, if this is the case, how does meaning ever originate? Lacan occasionally mistakenly equates this question with the problem of a certain 'paradox of meaning'. If each word is only definable in terms of other words, and these words in turn can only be defined in terms of still other words, how does any word receive a meaning in the first place? Some philosophers would halt the regress by positing certain basic words which need no definition in terms of further words – words, for instance, that can be defined ostensively by a simple pointing to the object denoted; others would claim that the regress is only apparent, based on a false initial presupposition, that the meaning of a word is to be understood in terms of its definition.

However, this is beside the point. The regress presumes that a signifier, or word, is fixed to its signified, or meaning: that a word means this rather than that, and that this particular meaning can only be set forth by means of other words. But it is precisely this notion that 'a word means this' which Lacan denies. A very crude analogy may help. Each player in a cricket team performs a role, and is given a formal title associated with the performance of that role: for example, 'wicket-keeper', 'first slip', 'bowler'. Now, arguably, it is not possible fully to explain what a particular position involves other than by relating it to other positions (for example, 'the first slip stands adjacent to the wicket-keeper, and on that side determined by the left-handedness or right-handedness of the receiving batsman'). Though this 'definitional regress' might be seen as problematic, it in no way involves the additional, and quite different claim, that 'wicket-keeper', 'first slip' and 'bowler', could fulfil one another's role and retain their original title. Playing this particular game involves interrelated positions, each of which, nevertheless, is fixed by means of a certain title. In Saussurean terms, meaningfully speaking a particular language (playing by its rules) involves the use of interrelated *signs*, each of which, nevertheless, consists of a fixed signifier–signified dyad.

Lacan is arguing for the interrelatedness of *signifiers*. These, in their entirety, can 'slide' over the signified. A word can mean anything, provided only that all the other words in the lexicon mean something different. But this is simply a situation in which communication is precluded, and, indeed, in which it is impossible to talk about meaning at all. How can we talk about signifieds (which presumably are discrete, differentiated concepts) unless we have the means to indicate them? In terms of the analogy, it is as if Lacan were presuming there was a game of cricket with its rules and various different positions, but then adding that these latter could be given any of the names available within the cricket playing lexicon. How to explain to someone what a 'wicket-keeper' does when this might mean any position on the field? Indeed, the whole idea of positions on the field becomes incomprehensible if a Lacanian 'sliding' of names over positions is conceded.

Laplanche is aware of Lacan's 'problem' only to the extent of seeking some point in the chain of signifiers where a signifier and signified are pinned together, and where, consequently, a vertical line, so to speak, attaches the signifying chain to the chain of signifieds. Laplanche's concept of the 'anchoring point' implies that there is a point in time at which certain signifiers become fixed to certain signifieds. It is as if cricket assumed the form of a meaningful game once the title 'wicket-keeper' meant its holder performed one and one only role on the field.

Lacan wants to deny any such 'anchorage', or fixed binding of signifier to signified, both within conscious language, and between this and the unconscious. However, his remarks on a putative chronological point of anchorage are elliptical. He cites the nursery rhyme, 'the dog goes miaow, the cat goes woof-woof', and comments that the child, by disconnecting the animal from its cry, raises the sign to the function of the signifier. The point would appear to be that the child breaks a natural, in this case onomatopoeic, relationship between what is named, the animal's distinguishing noise, and the name itself. It thus accedes to the realm of language proper, that is, signifiers whose relationship to the signified or real is arbitrary. But this is totally unconvincing. Let us conceive of 'miaow' as signifying the idea of mewing, and 'woof-woof' the idea of barking. Nonsense doggerel as quoted is nonsense precisely because certain qualities are incongruously or ludicrously attributed of certain objects. It is nonsense in this case because dogs do not mew and cats do not bark, but then 'miaow' certainly means mewing and 'woof-woof' certainly means barking. What the child imaginatively severs is the perceived real relationship between a type of animal and its typical sound, not that between the name for the (idea of the) sound and the (idea of the) sound itself.

To make his point Lacan uses a case where a putatively original relationship between signifier and signified is, as Saussure would express it, motivated, that is, non-arbitrary. The signifier mimics the signified (understood as the real object). Lacan presumably wishes to maintain that the signifier proper is arbitrary, having no 'natural' link with the signified. But this is culpably to play on different senses of 'natural' and 'necessary'. There is, of course, a 'natural' relationship, one of imitation, between the phoneme 'miaow', and the actual sound characteristic of cats. But there is no 'natural' relationship between 'miaow' and the *idea* of mewing, as indeed there is no natural relationship between any word, *qua* word, and any concept, *qua* concept. Moreover, to recapitulate a point made several times in both this chapter and Chapter 3: to maintain that there is necessarily a link between signifier and signified is not to be committed to the view that the link is one of natural or logical necessity. It is enough to claim that there are social rules whereby signifiers do have the meanings they have. Of course, we can speculate as to why these signifiers do have these meanings, and even imagine their having completely different meanings. The relationship between this signifier and its signified is contingent: it could have been other than it is. But, the fact remains that, at this particular moment in a particular language, particular

100

signifiers do mean particular things. And this claim does not necessarily entail any implausible belief in an original act of fixing signifiers to their meanings. The idea that language commences by a primitive naming exercise in which sounds or letters are appended to things or ideas is a myth rejected, not only by Lacan, but by all philosophers and linguists, whatever their persuasion. In sum, the fact that words do have the meanings they do is not invalidated by our having to uncover an original experience of nomination, nor, finally, our inability to discern a 'natural' relationship between words and meanings.

Unlike Lacan, Laplanche recognizes the need for language to have an anchorage. Thus, Laplanche's assumption of a certain fixity of meaning leads him to describe metaphor as the process whereby *new* meaning is generated. Lacan, on the other hand, tends to view metaphor as the fundamental operation whereby meaning as such is created. If meaning does not reside in the stable relationship of one signifier to a signified, then it can only be produced by and in the interrelationship *between* signifiers – the replacement of one by another, the shift from one to another. In this respect, note that, in the formula for metaphor cited in Chapter 3, 's', standing for a signified, only appeared on the right-hand side of the formula, being the product not the premiss of metaphor. This is required by Lacan's doctrine of the 'primacy of the signifier', but is ultimately incoherent. It is rather like saying that we could get to understand what each member of the fielding side does merely by an incantatory repetition of the names 'wicket-keeper', 'bowler', 'first slip' and so on. Laplanche is driven by his recognition of Lacan's problem to find an image for language's stability (i.e. that words do have fixed meanings). The point is that Lacan's 'problem' should be recognized as a refutation of his theory of language.

For Laplanche, such a stability is provided by a chain of unconscious signifiers, such that the unconscious can be said to be the condition for conscious language. More than anything else, it is this claim which directly inverts the central intuition of Lacan's thought. For Lacan, it is language which is the condition of the unconscious. For Laplanche, there can be no stable language without an unconscious; for Lacan, on the contrary, there can be no unconscious without language. Laplanche is led to distinguish between an unconscious and a conscious language; for Lacan there is only one level, that of the signifier. It is the sense absent from conscious discourse, its gaps or lacunae, which points us towards another chain of signifiers. These are not the Laplanchean elementary signifiers which are literally inscribed in another place, the unconscious. Lacan's answer to the problem of 'double inscription' is that the same signifier can play a double role according to whether it is part of conscious discourse or of a chain of unconscious associations. A simple example: in the sentence, 'Signorelli, Botticelli and Boltraffio are Italian painters', the signifiers 'Signorelli', 'Botticelli' and 'Boltraffio' have a function which is quite distinct from that they have in the unconscious chain of associations which make 'Botticelli' and 'Boltraffio' substitutes for the repressed 'Signorelli'. Further, it is only by attending to these signifiers *as* signifiers, that is as letters, that we are able to fill in the links missing from conscious discourse.

In the last analysis, it is because Laplanche takes the Freudian topography seriously and seeks to give a sense to the notion of the unconscious as another place, that he is led to speak of the unconscious as a 'language' distinct from but founding conscious language. Whereas for Lacan, the unconscious is the other side of conscious discourse, not another set of signifiers but another direction in which the same signifiers point. Laplanche's account may well be a serious misreading of Lacan, but it may nevertheless be an improvement.

It may well be that it is his very fidelity to Freud which makes him unfaithful to Lacan; and, ironically, his misplaced fidelity to Lacan in certain fundamental respects that reveals the incoherence of any theory founded upon the 'primacy of the signifier'.

Notes

1   André Green, 'L'Inconscient freudien et la psychoanalyse française contemporaine', *Les Temps modernes*, no. 195 (August 1962), p. 372, n. 14.

2   'The Unconscious: a psychoanalytic study', *Yale French Studies*, no. 48 (1972), p. 153.

3   ibid., p. 161.

4   Compare 'The Unconscious', *SE*, XIV, p. 199 and 'A metapsychological supplement to the theory of dreams', *SE*, XIV, p. 229.

5   'Repression', *SE*, XIV, p. 153.

Further reading

Laplanche's and Leclaire's article originally appeared as 'L'Inconscient: une étude psychanalytique' in *Les Temps modernes*, no. 183 (July 1961), pp. 81–129. The English translation, 'The Unconscious: a psychoanalytic study', was published in *Yale French Studies*, no. 48, pp. 118–75.

André Green has provided a summary of the Bonneval conference, 'Les portes de l'inconscient' in *L'Inconscient* (VIth Colloque de Bonneval) (Paris 1966), and the same author offers a critique of Laplanche and Leclaire, stressing their neglect of the economic point of view, in 'L'Inconscient freudien et la psychanalyse française contemporaine', *Les Temps modernes*, no. 195 (August 1962), pp. 365–79.

The main source for Lacan's views on Laplanche and Leclaire is his 'Preface' to, and reported conversation as an Appendix in, Anika Lemaire's *Jacques Lacan* (translated by David Macey (London 1977)). Lemaire gives over Parts 4 and 5 of her book to a careful critical appraisal of Laplanche's and Leclaire's ideas. It errs only in uncritically assuming a Lacanian position from which to attack the errors of Laplanche and Leclaire.

Lacan's comments on the *points de capiton* can be found in 'The subversion of the subject and the dialectic of desire in the Freudian unconscious', in *Écrits, A Selection* (translated by Alan Sheridan (London 1977)), pp. 303 ff.

Lacan's repudiation of the views of Laplanche and Leclaire was very confusing for those English-speaking critics who previously had used the latter to understand the former. For a good example of such confusion see the two versions of Martin Thom's 'The Unconscious structured as a language', *Economy & Society*, **5** (1976), pp. 435–69; and in Colin McCabe (ed.), *The Talking Cure, Essays in Psychoanalysis and Language* (London 1981), pp. 1–44.

5

Timpanaro's critique

The previous chapters have all taken the Freudian notion of 'the unconscious' seriously. To this extent: Sartre's critique has been represented as a misconstrual of Freudian theory, in that it fails adequately to take account of the radical heterogeneity of unconscious and conscious. No satisfactory explanation of a subject's misrecognition of their utterances and deeds could be given in existentialist terms by means of the conceptual opacity of a nevertheless translucent self-consciousness. The sense in which this opaqueness or misrecognition could be understood at the level of language was explored through the work of Lacan, Laplanche and Leclaire. It was concluded that, in so far as such writing presupposed something like the 'primacy of the signifier', it made linguistic sense of Freud at the expense of making nonsense of language.

However, nothing in this would preclude there being *some sense* of the Freudian unconscious which was both coherent and true. In Sartrean terms, we are left with the *facts* of the Freudian 'discovery' and unresolved doubts about the proffered forms of explanation. In Chapter 1 I suggested that Freudian theory contained an unhappy amalgam of biological and mentalistic languages, with the further suggestion that this ambiguity resulted from the combination of two incompatible theories of mind.

I will now consider a critique of Freud which vigorously and openly disputes the purported 'factual' demonstration of the existence of 'the unconscious'. This is provided by Sebastiano Timpanaro in his book, *The Freudian Slip*. Timpanaro contends that Freud begs the question of the existence of 'the unconscious' by his very mode of explanation. Timpanaro does not, however, attempt a systematic and comprehensive refutation of Freudianism. Rather, by restricting himself to an analysis of an exemplary Freudian text, *The Psychopathology of Everyday Life*, he seeks to demonstrate the inadequacy of Freud's methodology and the redundancy of certain key theoretical notions. Timpanaro proposes alternative, and more economical, explanations of those examples which serve Freud's 'demonstration' of the 'facts' of repression and the existence of the unconscious. Further, he attempts to show how Freud forces his own interpretation at the expense of these alternatives and to the neglect of other relevant evidence. In direct contrast with Lacan, Timpanaro claims that psychoanalytic method rests upon a misunderstanding and misuse of linguistics and theories of discourse.

A proper appreciation of Timpanaro's work is complicated by a simple fact: Timpanaro writes as a Marxist attacking Freudian theory for its failure to be either materialist or scientific. His work has been published in translation by a leading Left-wing British publisher. That in itself would not necessarily be significant were it not for the further fact that Freudianism, and in particular Lacanianism, has played a significant contributory role in the formation of certain kinds of contemporary Marxist theory. In attacking Freud, Timpanaro is well aware of those 'behind' Freud who will recognize where his criticism is aimed. As a result, the dialogue – what little there has been – between Timpanaro and his critics has, unfortunately, been at the level of an anti-Freudian Marxist debating with Freudian Marxists. This has led to obfuscation, and, to a large degree, the replacement of argument by accusation.

Of course, if the Lacanian or Freudian theory of the unconscious is characterized as essential to an enrichment of Marxism, then clearly it matters if the former can be shown to be defective, false or incoherent. However, such failings would matter to *anyone* – Marxist or otherwise – who espoused such a theory. Again, Timpanaro, as a Marxist, may err in using or assuming certain postulates by which to criticize Freud. But, first, it is wrong to suppose that there are agreed 'Marxist' critical postulates; and, second, not all of Timpanaro's criticism begs the question of what constitutes a correct Marxist explanation. Indeed, it is ironic that Timpanaro's most consistent and sustained critical attack makes no such assumptions, relying as it does on his other scientific allegiance – to philology. The respects in which Timpanaro's book are weakest are precisely those in which he offers a somewhat stipulative definition of Marxism by which Freudianism is found wanting. These concern the notions of 'materialism' and 'science'. Of the first, the following can be said now. There is no reason why a 'materialist' (in Timpanaro's sense) should necessarily be a Marxist. That Marxists should be materialists, in this sense, is the much disputed claim of Timpanaro's other major text, and beyond the scope of this book.

Nevertheless, it is curious that Lacanian theory should have been adopted by some writers for the purposes of developing a 'materialist understanding of the subject'. As has been shown, Lacan's interpretation of Freud is notable for its neglect of the latter's materialism. And there is no evidence that those who profess to use Lacan in a 'materialist' way are prepared to deal with any of the problems of materialism discussed so far. To that extent Timpanaro's commitment to materialism is instructive. His criticisms draw attention to the character of Freud's own professed materialism, and relate directly to remarks made earlier in this book.

However, Timpanaro's central criticisms of Freud owe nothing to his materialist commitment. The bulk of his critical exposé of Freud concentrates upon two examples from *The Psychopathology of Everyday Life*. One, the forgetting of 'Signorelli', has already been cited in Chapter 3. The other occurs in Chapter 2 of Freud's text and concerns a young man's inability, in Freud's presence, to remember a line from Virgil. In particular, he forgets the word 'aliquis'. At Freud's suggestion, the young man freely associates to the missed word. Eventually, he arrives at the thought, which he confesses to Freud, that he is currently preoccupied with his mistress's missed period and the consequent fear that she might be pregnant.

Among the more striking of the associative links are the following: 'aliquis' suggests both *reliquien* (relics) and *liquefying*; there comes into the young man's thoughts the names of saints. One of these, St Janarius, is associated with a purported miracle whereby his blood miraculously liquefies on a certain holy day, any delay in this event occasioning much excitement among the expectant faithful. For Freud, these freely associated thoughts uncover an intimate connection between a repressed topic, the fear lest the mistress be pregnant, and the missing word. The entire Virgil line from the *Aeneid* expresses the desire of Dido for descendants who may avenge her. The young man employed it to conclude an impassioned statement on the frustrations suffered by his generation. But, while consciously expressing such a wish for children, the unconscious wish for the exact contrary, arising from the fear that he might well soon have a child, obtruded. The unconscious wish thus disturbed the consciously intended quotation, and disturbed it precisely at that point, the word 'aliquis', wherein associative links from the repressed topic could be effected.

Timpanaro proposes an alternative explanation of the young man's misquotation, and denies that the example demonstrates any causal relationship between an unconscious wish and the word's omission. Timpanaro's explanation employs the philological notion of 'banalization', the replacement of archaic and unusual linguistic forms with those more familiar to the speaker and in common use. This may be effected by a reduction, expansion or alteration of the original text. Evidence in abundance of this process can be found in the history of textual transcriptions, and indeed in the colloquial use of famous misquotations. English language instances of the latter might include, 'make assurance *doubly* [instead of the correct *double*] sure', 'I escaped *by* [instead of the correct *with*] the skin of my teeth'. It is not surprising to Timpanaro that Freud's young companion should have banalized the Virgil quotation, which was anomalous even in its Latin construction, and which, to such a person, would have been no more than a vaguely remembered part of an earlier classical education. Moreover, the omission of 'aliquis' is understandable in so far as this particular word is not crucial to the entire sentence's meaning. Without this indefinite pronoun, 'aliquis', the quoted sentence still conveys the essential sense desired by the young man, whatever the damage done to its metre.

Before considering Timpanaro's response to Freud's evidence of a specifically psychoanalytic link between a putative repressed thought and the omission of a word, let us examine his alternative explanation of the 'Signorelli' example. Once again Timpanaro draws on his philological training to explain the replacement of 'Signorelli' by 'Botticelli'/ 'Boltraffio' as an instance of a common enough error of textual transcription – a confusion between words of identical syllabic number and some phonetic similarity. Botticelli's assonance with Signorelli makes it an admirable substitute, all the more so in that both name Italian Renaissance painters of the same historical period. As for the name, 'Boltraffio', which subsequently enters Freud's mind, Timpanaro suggests that this fits the process of 'disimprovement', that is, an unsuccessful attempt to rectify what is recognized as an initial mistake. Knowing Botticelli to be incorrect, Freud 'disimproves' upon it in his attempt to achieve Signorelli; he falsely isolates the initial mistake in the last rather than the first element of the word. As before, Timpanaro cites similar examples from the tradition of textual copying to substantiate his claim.

Of course, a defender of Freud will readily concede that textual corruptions such as banalization and disimprovement exist. However, they will insist that, given the weight of psychoanalytic evidence provided by the discerned associative links between unconscious thought and omitted or substituted words, such philological explanations cannot be comprehensive. At most, they can serve only to specify the linguistic conditions which facilitate, rather than cause, the error in question. Indeed, Freud himself was not unaware of alternative causal explanations of slips of the form offered by Timpanaro. However, he chose to regard these as specifying the circumstances favouring the commission, but providing neither necessary nor sufficient conditions, of the error. A complete causal account of the slip requires the discovery of a repressed unconscious wish or thought, and this is indicated by the associative links which relate it to the error in question.

Now talk of a distinction between 'favouring circumstances' and 'cause proper' is somewhat loose, and things are not helped when defenders of Freud misuse his notion of 'overdetermination'. Any particular event, Z, is produced, or brought about, by a set of antecedent causal conditions, $A, B, C, D, \ldots$ etc., which are individually necessary and jointly sufficient for the occurrence of Z. Let Z be a particular slip, and let A, B, C, D, E and F specify the various conditions covered by non-Freudian explanations of such a slip. The Freudian claim appears to be that these are necessary for ('circumstances favouring') the occurrence of the slip, but not sufficient. Also necessary is G, the presence of an unconscious wish. Of course, A to G are all 'causes' of Z. The sense in which G is the 'cause proper' is not just that, without G, Z would not occur (the same may well be true of A to F), but that only G 'makes sense of' Z. That is, Z, being the particular slip it is, is related to G, as the particular unconscious wish it is, in a way that does not apply to the former's relation to $A \ldots F$: namely by means of discerned associative links. It is, however, mistaken to speak of Z as overdetermined by A to G. Overdetermination, in the Freudian sense, refers to the fact that a single symptom, parapraxis, or whatever, is related to more than one *unconscious element*. So, A to F are causal antecedent conditions favouring the production of A; G, G', G'' are unconscious wishes, ideas, etc. overdetermining the particular sense of Z.

A couple of remarks are in order. First, some Freudians see no problem in characterizing some at least of A to F as somatic or physio-logical states, while specifying that G, G', G'' are unconscious *psychic* elements. Not for the first time, we are left with the unresolved and unexplained combination of mental and physical factors in a causal account. Second, some defenders of Freud appear to suggest that A to F are not sufficient to explain other factors co-attendant upon the occur-rence of the slip – for instance, the subjects' irritation at forgetting, their certainty of having made a mistake – and implicitly claim that G is necessary for an explanation of these facts also. This may be true, but it requires extensive additional argument. It is not inconceivable that a comprehensive causal explanation could be given of the psychological state accompanying the commission of a slip which did not have to postulate unconscious elements of the Freudian kind. Moreover, few Freudians sustain their counter claim, and are content to let the weight of their argument rest upon the notion of 'making sense of the slip'. That is, what is defective about non-Freudian explanations of parapraxes is that they fail to show both why this particular slip occurred, and why it can have a sense in relation to its postulated main cause, the uncon-scious element(s).

Timpanaro denies the existence of any such causal relation (between slip and unconscious element(s)) in the examples cited, and maintains that the associative links supposedly uncovered provide little, if any, confirmation of such a putative relation. Timpanaro's comments on both the 'aliquis' and the 'Signorelli' examples echo those of other critics unsympathetic to Freud who believe they discern an alarming arbitrariness in the associations. One index of this arbitrariness, for Timpanaro, is that, by means of psychoanalytic association, one can apparently link anything – an idea, word, or memory – to any other thing (Ludwig Wittgenstein is reported to have remarked that, using the 'logic' of free association, one could start with any of a collection of objects on a table and find that they were all connected in a pattern).[1] Indeed, Timpanaro suggests that any of the other three words in the Virgil line could serve as a point of departure and lead, by means of an associative relation, to the topic of the unwanted pregnancy. Such an arbitrariness of association would seem to preclude the rigid causal determination of symptom or slip by the repressed thought to which Freud was undoubtedly committed.

The reply by Freudians tends to be twofold. First, it is denied that the relation between repressed thought and error is exactly equivalent,

though in reversed direction, to that uncovered through free association. Second, the 'arbitrariness', or better 'artificiality', of the associative connections is admitted by Freud, who explicitly speaks of 'forced
and far-fetched' links. However, such an artificiality is precisely characteristic of the unconscious primary process which obeys laws essentially
different from those of conscious ratiocination and the secondary
process. The force of the first reply would be that any apparent causal
anomaly in the analytic reconstruction of the symptomatic error does
not incriminate the causal relation operating in the formation of this
error; the force of the second that this relation can be understood only in
terms of a causality that is peculiar and proper to the unconscious itself.

Of the first claim the textual evidence from Freud does not provide
unambiguous confirmation. Freud certainly believed that any 'retracing' of the path from the repressed thought to the symptom is complicated by the fact that further material intervenes between the time of
symptom formation and the time of its analytic reconstruction. This
additional material will be compounded of fresh associative links and
heightened resistances. However, Freud seems to suggest that such
later additions are themselves a direct function of the original associative relations, providing in fact short-circuits between the originally
laid down connecting thoughts.[2] It is one thing to maintain that the
analytic process constructs an entirely new relation between symptom
and repressed to that of the former's formation; quite another that the
original relation is the basis of later short-circuiting complications.
Timpanaro quite legitimately points out that the 'free' which qualifies
association implies only the analysand's relaxation of the conscious
critical control of his or her thoughts, and not an absence of psychic
determination. There is no sense in which Freud regards such association as merely random utterances by which one is 'lucky enough' to
chance eventually upon the repressed topic. Indeed, the assurance
Freud frequently expressed at having reached the repressed thought
was given by the determinant character of the analytic 'retracing' of the
path of symptom formation.

In a footnote added in 1920 to *The Psychopathology of Everyday Life* (*SE*,
VI, p. 250 n. 2) Freud considers the evidence of experiments with
associations from numbers. A certain experimenter found that he and
his subjects were able to produce associations to numbers that were
chosen at random. These associations had all the appearance of having
determined the choice of the presented number. While accepting that

Schneider's findings could apply equally to word association, Freud denies Schneider's overall conclusion that the emergence of associations fails to show any causal relation between them and a spontaneously occurring, rather than randomly presented, number or word: 'the fact that appropriate associations arise to numbers (or words) which are *presented* tells us nothing more about the origin of numbers (or words) which emerge *spontaneously* than could be taken into consideration before that fact was known'. Freud supplies no further argument to show why the two cases should be regarded differently. Indeed, he admits that psychoanalytic investigation proceeds on the 'presupposition' that the spontaneously produced word is determined by the thoughts disclosed by free association during analysis.

Of course, an immediate reply is that such a presupposition is precisely what Freud ought to have proved, and that, consequently, his whole approach is question-begging or circular. Why not presuppose that the associations to a randomly chosen word determine *its* appearance? After all, such associations share with those to a spontaneously occurring word the appearance of determining the word. It is not inconceivable that someone should be presented with the word, 'aliquis', asked to freely associate and, coincidentally, arrive by means of association at the confessed thought that he was worried about his girlfriend's missed period. It would, of course, be absurd to conclude that this fear determined the choice of the word, 'aliquis', and yet such associations in this case might well display the same 'logical' form, if not an exactly similar content, to those produced by Freud's young student. Freud would need to provide arguments that either ruled out such a hypothetical possibility on principle or showed it to differ in significant respects from his own example. Neither seem forthcoming.

Freudians may point out that the imputed circularity is not vicious in so far as the presupposition is productive of new knowledge. It is only by assuming that there *is* an, as yet unknown, repressed thought responsible for the slip that we are led down labyrinthine paths we would otherwise forbear to travel to the disclosure of the particular repressed topic in question. In other words, it is surely significant that we do arrive at something previously unacknowledged but which, subsequent to the analytic process of free association, is admitted by the analysand. The young man is led, by means of free association, from his forgetting of 'aliquis' to the confession before Freud of a real worry concerning his mistress's possible pregnancy. Surely this confirms the existence of some intimate connection between the omission and the repressed thought, and suggests that the former served to conceal the latter.

Timpanaro makes a number of points against such an assumption. In the first place, it is proper to qualify the value of the analysand's avowal. There is an important difference between an admission by the analysand of the possession of certain thoughts and an acceptance by the same person of the 'sense' of Freud's interpretation. The first-person avowal by the student of his having a particular worry must, in the circumstances, be accepted at face value. However, the student is not in a similarly privileged position with respect to any confirmation of a causal link between this thought and his forgetting of 'aliquis'. The reason which Freud supplies for the student's forgetting does not have the character of an intention, of which he was at the time aware and to which he subsequently can admit. Rather it is a putative causal explanation, evidence for which the student may indeed supply, but whose validity as an explanation he is in no better position than anyone else to confirm.

Moreover, there are good reasons why the student should readily have accepted Freud's interpretation. We are told that he was familiar with Freud's writings, and sufficiently impressed by his work to request an explanation of his forgetfulness. Before the free association commences, the student accepts that there must be some Freudian reason for his misremembering of the quotation. In other words, he is predisposed from the outset to accept the interpretation Freud 'uncovers', and this is only compounded by his ignorance of those other kinds of possible explanation which Timpanaro himself seeks to reinstate. Timpanaro is perhaps overkeen to discern an authoritarianism implicit in the analyst–analysand relationship, and to underline the suggestive interferences of Freud himself in the supposedly 'free' associations. For Timpanaro, there is a very pregnant sense in which the student is 'led' from 'aliquis' to the confessed worry.

It will matter to some extent if the analysands' associations are not entirely and unambiguously their own, but, in significant measure, suggested by the analyst to already suggestible analysands. But, in the last analysis, the crucial point is not that the patient's consent to Freud's interpretation is 'coerced', but that such consent, however obtained, has little or no confirmatory value. Someone may, with delighted surprise, confirm the personal facts that a palmist 'reads' in their hands, but that does not validate the procedures of palmistry itself.

Nevertheless, to pursue the analogy, the palmist does arrive at confirmed personal knowledge of his or her clients, which we might presume them initially not to have. Similarly, the psychoanalytic procedure of free association does produce a confession, and, moreover, by taking as its starting point what most people, certainly prior to Freud's researches, would regard as a trivial or unimportant verbal slip. Timpanaro points to certain features of the 'aliquis' example which make this version of events less than compelling. The student's confession is not difficult to secure and it would be inappropriate to describe his anxiety as hidden deep within the unconscious, or indeed as genuinely repressed. It should be noted that the 'Signorelli' and 'aliquis' examples, so often cited as impressive and convincing demonstrations of the unconscious's existence, both concern 'repressed' topics whose inherent seriousness does not prevent their owners coming to avow them with a remarkable lack of significant resistance. In the 'aliquis' case, the reported conversation suggests that, to use the colloquial English, the worry was at the back of the student's mind all along. The conversation has the form of a small, enclosed, tale with its prologue, dialogue and happy Freudian ending. On such minimal literary evidence it is dangerous to speculate as to the student's motives and attitudes – as Timpanaro is perhaps prone to do. Yet it is not inconceivable that the young man welcomed the opportunity to unburden himself of a problem currently demanding his attention, that knowing of Freud's work and respecting him as a distinguished elder, he should find his way round to sharing a confidence which currently oppressed him. Wanting to disclose the secret, and yet aware of conversational proprieties, the mini-analysis provided the student with the perfect alibi for such a disclosure, and one whose form was extremely satisfying for, and flattering of, the listener, Freud.

This is perhaps extravagant speculation. The point is that in this case, as in others, we should not be surprised that an individual's preoccupation with a trouble or serious matter leads him or her to find a means to disclose it. Nor, therefore, should we be surprised that a bizarre associational 'logic' appears to lead ineluctably from a trivial error to its disclosure. The only surprise is that Freudians should interpret this associational pathway as irrefutable evidence of a unique causal relation. Nothing in Timpanaro's denial of a causal link between the forgotten word and the repressed thought entails a denial of causes for both the forgetfulness and the avowal of the repressed worry.

However, given all of the foregoing, nothing in Freud's account warrants an ascription of causality to the coincidental and associational connection between the two. There are available equally good, if not better, alternative reasons why the student made the verbal slip, why he confessed his worry, and why he was able to produce an associative relation between the slip and the worry.

Let us now return to the second reply that Freudians might make to Timpanaro's argument: that the 'arbitrariness' of the associational links between the repressed thought and the symptom or parapraxis implies not the absence of any causal relation, but rather the presence of a peculiar kind of causal relation, one proper to unconscious processes. To complicate matters, it is pointed out that there can be a direct relation between the repressed thought and disturbed utterance. In the 'aliquis' example, there is a comprehensible link between the unconscious wish that the mistress should not be pregnant and the conscious wish, expressed in the Virgil quotation, for children. Indeed, having initially suggested that the 'Signorelli' example differs significantly in displaying no such relation, Freud speculates, in a footnote, whether there might not in fact be a similar direct link between the forgetting of 'Signorelli' and the figurative representation of the repressed topic (death and sexuality) in this painter's recently visited Orvieto frescoes: 'The Four Last Things' (Death, Judgement, Hell and Heaven). Consequently, if there is any 'arbitrariness', it characterizes not the relationship as such between repressed thought and disturbed quotation, which is 'essential', 'necessary' and 'internal', but the manner or form of the actual link effected, which is 'arbitrary', 'roundabout' and 'external'. What appears anomalous is not *that* the quotation is disturbed, but that it is disturbed at one particular point and in particular ways.

Now, first it is clear that, for Freud, the existence of such an 'internal' relation is not necessary. There are cases where the only relationship between the repressed thought and the disturbed quotation is that 'externally' effected by roundabout associational links. The repressed topic just happens to be temporally contiguous with the topic of the intended utterance; the latter is not disturbed because it conveys a sense in contradiction with, or otherwise related to, that of the repressed thought. Second, even if there are good unconscious reasons why an utterance should be disturbed, it remains satisfactorily to be explained why the quotation is disturbed in precisely the way it is. After all, a simple transformation of the Virgil quotation, 'Let someone arise from

114

my bones as an Avenger', into its contrary, 'Let no one . . .', would have accorded with the sense of the unconscious fear and exemplified a type of verbal slip Freud was fond of citing. (The President of the Lower House who, presumably expecting little from the forthcoming session, declared it closed instead of open, is one instance.) Why then, with 'aliquis', as in so many other instances, should the unconscious adopt such a devious and complicated means of expressing itself?

To this question, Freud offers a twofold reply, both terms of which Timpanaro finds objectionable and unscientific. First, the sense of any particular symptom is ultimately susceptible to a complete explanation only in terms of the individual patient's particular experiences and past history. We cannot say that a fear lest one's girlfriend be pregnant will always, and for every person, produce a forgetting of the word 'aliquis'. In the cited case, this is dependent upon the young student's specific circumstances: his past history and present situation. Second, unconscious formations strike us as aberrant and anomalous only because of our attachment to forms of conscious thinking which the unconscious scorns to observe.

In the first reply Timpanaro finds evidence of a tendency towards individualizing explanation which he believes to be fundamentally inconsistent with the requisite generality of a genuine scientific interpretation. Timpanaro overstates his case by polemical resort to a distinction between 'abstract' science and 'concrete' magic. The objection cannot be to individual descriptions as such, but only to the purportedly scientific use made of them. For, on the one hand, a causal explanation of an individual event could be described as rigorously scientific if it is prescribed, in principle, that a repetition of certain specified antecedent causal conditions would lead to the occurrence of the same event. It is not necessary that, in practice, the event ever should reoccur. On the other hand, instances of a general causal law may have to be explained with reference to their particular and distinguishing features. After all, if 'exposure to extreme cold is likely to induce frostbite in an otherwise healthy individual' is analogous to 'the presence of unconscious wishes is likely to produce slips of the tongue in otherwise normal individuals', it is no more inappropriate to ask with respect to the first claim, 'why did this individual contract such a severe/slight case of frostbite and with such additional complications?', than it is to inquire on the basis of the second, 'why did this individual make this particular slip in these particular circumstances?'.

Timpanaro's real objection is that the individual descriptions of Freudian psychoanalysis do not function in a way consonant with the practice of good science. The law-like claim, 'Every slip is the result of an unconscious wish's interference with consciously intended discourse', is, for Timpanaro, 'confirmed' by so describing every individual slip that an unconscious wish is found responsible for its occurrence. And this is made possible by allowing any association to count as a determining link between unconscious wish and slip. Thus, in response to the second Freudian defence quoted above, Timpanaro claims that the 'alogicality' of the unconscious is characterized in a way that precludes nothing from counting as an explanatory association. It is, of course, quite legitimate to maintain that unconscious thought processes are rule governed, but with rules that differ radically and essentially from those governing conscious thought processes. It is quite another matter if the unconscious processes possess no rules of any sort, and if there are no limits to what can be said to be an association produced by the unconscious. Normal linguistic or logical relations may indeed be inadequate to describe the properties of unconscious thought processes. But it does not follow that there should be no relations adequate to such a description.

Thus Timpanaro cannot discern any specification of that 'code' which would make it proper to speak of a 'language' peculiar to the unconscious. Of course, Lacanians will respond that the unconscious does display a specific and a specifiable form of linguistic organization, one subsumed under the 'primacy of the signifier'. This may mean, as seen in Chapter 3, that the unconscious follows the rules of metaphor and metonymy, comprehending a signifier only in its relation to other signifiers. However, as Timpanaro points out, there are examples, embarrassing for such an interpretation, of 'normal' unconscious ratiocination and association: the conjunction of saints in the 'aliquis' case, and of 'Bosnia' and 'Herzegovina' in the 'Signorelli' case, depend upon relations between signifieds. Indeed, there are many other instances in Freud's writings of associational links and symbolic substitutions which employ factual, semantic and visual similarities or oppositions between signifieds. It is not here a question of the unconscious breaking the rules of conscious language. The unconscious violates the counterrules imputed to it.

Moreover, the unconscious frequently appears to demonstrate a linguistic sophistication and facility, which differs from conscious performance only in its degree of improvement upon the latter. In speaking of a 'polyglot unconscious', Timpanaro draws attention to the impressive bi-, even multi-lingualism, of the unconscious – whose capacity for surprisingly exact, and frequently erudite, translation appears strangely at odds with its purported primitivism and deviancy from any normal conscious command of language. It is not just that an individual's unconscious is comfortably conversant with many languages (and often obscure literary and cultural sources). It is so in many cases where the conscious individual can hardly be presumed to have such knowledge. The young student should not worry at his conscious misremembering of Virgil, his unconscious displays a compensating and impressive fluency in Italian and French.

Those Freudians who reply that the unconscious is not accountable before the court of reason, and that we should only ask ourselves for whom such linguistic excellence is considered so extraordinary, would seem to take their final stand on the ground of mysticism. The unconscious does indeed move in a mysterious way and some Freudian defences of the concept of the unconscious resemble theological defences of wonders performed by God. For both, it is improper to regard the concept as eligible for the normal processes of rational or logical demonstration.

Timpanaro's critique of the Freudian unconscious thus differs significantly from others, like Sartre's, which merely purports to show that Freud *misexplains* the demonstrated facts. For Timpanaro, the Freudian unconscious both *overexplains* and *underexplains*. The point is this: Sartre does not, in a way, deny that there is both a 'conscious' phenomenon and an 'unconscious' desire, belief or idea to which the former is related. Sartre's claim is that this relation cannot sensibly be read as causal; and, if it must therefore be understood as intentional, then we should employ the notion of a single unitary consciousness rather than that of separated yet communicating psychic regions. 'Unconscious' can be made philosophically harmless and unobjectionable by being explicated as something like 'comprehended yet conceptually ungrasped'. Sartre would not perhaps deny that Freud's concern with death and sexuality explained his failure to remember 'Signorelli'; nor that the student's anxiety over his mistress's possible pregnancy made sense of his misquotation of Virgil. This is the measure of Sartre's agreement with the demonstrated 'facts' of Freudian cases. It is disagreement with the why and how of Freud's explanation that informs Sartre's critique proper.

For Timpanaro, on the other hand, there is a denial of the purported relation as such. He is prepared to concede that both Freud and the student did have their respective worries, and that, at the time of committing their respective parapraxes, they were not immediately aware of these anxieties. However, the worry is not needed to explain the slip, for the latter is completely comprehensible in purely philological terms. The associative links which 'demonstrate' the existence of the unconscious/consciousness relationship are pseudo-links achieved by an improper forcing of linguistic possibilities and the coerced, but anyway irrelevant, consent of the analysand to the interpretation.

This is the sense in which the Freudian unconscious overexplains, and thus explains nothing at all – by introducing a quite unnecessary realm of unconscious processes to which the anxieties in question purportedly belong, and then fabricating a series of connections between this realm and that of conscious processes. There is another sense in which Freud overexplains. Timpanaro concedes that there is a category of slip which is not susceptible of a purely philological explanation. What he terms *gaffes* covers those cases where the speaker involuntarily expresses something that is not, in the immediate circumstances, either intended or wished. The case of the President of the Lower House, cited earlier, is a good example. The problem for Freud is that, ironically, the very wealth of such examples – in literature and reflected in colloquial expressions – shows the gaffe to be a widespread and widely acknowledged phenomenon. There is, however, no need to have recourse to the dynamics of the repressed unconscious to explain such occurrences. Indeed, many of the gaffes which Freud quotes indicate the presence in their perpetrators of temporarily 'suppressed', but immediately acknowledged, desires, beliefs or attitudes. In the case of the gaffe, Freud's notion of the unconscious overexplains what is open to less convoluted psychological explanation. At most we would only require something akin to Freud's own notion of the preconscious. We would have little or no problem in accepting the sense of 'unconscious' in which someone might say: 'Good heavens, did I say that? I didn't mean to. What I meant to say was ". . .". But, of course, as you must realize and as I'm now aware, I was unconsciously thinking at the same time of. . . .'

Now Timpanaro seems prepared to concede that there are instances of *gaffes* which can, with some plausibility, be described in Freudian terms, that is, as the exploitation of certain linguistic possibilities. For instance, a Jewish convert to Christianity, acutely aware of, and anxious not to reveal, his Jewishness, referred to his children as *Juden* (Jews) not *jungen* (youngsters). Such a case fits a colloquial use of the term 'Freudian slip', whereby someone involuntarily and unintentionally 'gives themselves away'. However, Timpanaro's point is twofold. First, such cases do not require the forced and far-fetched associationalism typified in the 'Signorelli' and 'aliquis' cases; second, the unuttered thought which distorts the intended speech is either one of which the speaker is acutely aware or one which is properly described as merely suppressed. What Timpanaro really objects to is the purported existence of genuinely *repressed* material which can only be disclosed by means of the suspect 'logic' of analytic association.

If we use 'the unconscious' in the less contentious sense to denote the suppressed thoughts, desires and attitudes of which individuals would rather not be reminded, of which they strive not to be aware, then a productive area of psychological inquiry is opened. Moreover, such an inquiry would also be social – investigating the general historical and cultural conditions for the suppression of certain kinds of material. It is precisely in this respect that, for Timpanaro, the Freudian unconscious underexplains by failing to disclose those thoughts we might expect of such an unconscious.

Timpanaro believes it noteworthy that, among the repressed thoughts discerned by Freud, none concerned either the biological frailty of humans or class conflict. Not one of psychoanalysis's early patients was unconsciously anxious about the death of themselves – either as a biological individual or as a member of a historically threatened class. (The need for the second to be present is given by Timpanaro's own understanding of materialism, that of the first by some version of historical materialism.) Timpanaro thinks that such absences mean the Freudian account of bourgeois neuroses is seriously deficient. It is, of course, highly questionable to argue that, if the bourgeoisie did have unconscious thoughts, they should have been of a certain kind. Are we to blame the bourgeoisie for its lack of class-unconsciousness, or Freud for the incompleteness of his discovery of what really worried them?

If Timpanaro's charge has any merit, it lies in indicating the extent to which it might be thought profitable to give unpleasant, repressed, excluded and suppressed thoughts a historical context. Such an approach needs to be clarified. There are critics of Freud – most notably

Jung – who charge Freud with 'pan-sexualism', objecting thereby to the fact that Freud's unconscious is eternally and absolutely the domain for the representation of exclusively sexual instincts. Some might regard such a 'pan-sexualism' as determined by the historical conditions in which Freudian psychoanalysis was constituted as a new discipline. We have earlier quoted Sartre's remark to the effect that Freud singled out sexual need because his historical milieu was one in which that need predominated; in another epoch he might have chosen hunger as the foremost instinct. On the other hand, there are those Marxists who accept the predominance of the sexual instincts, but maintain that Freud erroneously universalized a notion of sexuality that was, in effect, specific to bourgeois patriarchal society; he falsely assumed that the nature of sexual repression was invariant between classes and epochs, and made the individual the fundamental basis of his aetiological inquiries. The above reproaches do not involve any denial that repression occurs, that something is forcibly excluded or expelled from conscious awareness. The disagreements with Freud concern exactly what is repressed and why.

There is, however, a different, and perhaps stronger, version of the 'historical context' argument, which maintains that the idea of 'repression' itself must be historically situated. We might, in this respect, very briefly mention the views of Michel Foucault on sexuality. For Foucault, psychoanalysis is a transformation of Christian confession, and belongs in its formation to those professional sciences of the human individual which constitute sexuality as the clandestine, excluded truth of man. The very idea of some innermost core, which is necessarily hidden, latent, forgotten and elusive, is argued to have a pre-history and, in its psychoanalytic form, to have a precise historical determination and political function. In a different fashion, Timpanaro advances the tentative suggestion that the idea of a repressed unconscious accorded well with the character of Freud's turn of the century, Viennese bourgeois clientele. Because of their background, these felt the need to do and say what was forbidden, to break the rules – and what better alibi for the gratification of such an impulse than the psychoanalytic claim that we are all the unwitting victims of unconscious desires which inform our very actions and words.

The foregoing is no more than speculative and schematic history of ideas. However, it is worth emphasizing the quite distinct points of 'historical' attack on the Freudian unconscious. For some, psychoanalysis remains a science whose genuine discovery and proper object of study is 'the unconscious' or 'the repressed'. What may need to be corrected are the class and historical 'biases' which are implicated in Freud's actual characterization of this object. For others, the psychoanalytic idea of a repressed unconscious has itself to be explained historically and shown to have specifiable origins.

In addition to his 'historical materialist' critique, Timpanaro accuses Freud of an equally fundamental anti-materialism. He argues, again in schematic fashion, that Freud's concept of the unconscious is vitiated by a crucial contradiction internal to the whole of his thought – that between the materialism of his scientific formation and the anti-materialist cultural, philosophical pretensions his work acquired. On the one hand, Freud's commitment to the determinism and materialism of his scientific teachers led him to understand the unconscious in fundamentally biological and neurophysiological terms, and to appreciate the need to deepen any theory of the sexual instincts by reference to a physiological and biochemical foundation. The distinction effected between the psychical and physiological was merely a temporary expedient essential to the foundation of a specifically psychological science. On the other hand, under the influence of such anti-materialist philosophical writers as Brentano, Schopenhauer and Nietzsche, the unconscious acquired an intentionality and personhood. The unconscious became the other side of the human psyche or spirit – timeless, primitive and irrational. Freud's commitment to a final reduction of psychic to neurophysiological terms was eventually only token. The gap opened between the psychical and biological was never closed; indeed, Timpanaro holds psychoanalysis responsible in large part for the dissolution of an original and productive relationship between psychology/psychiatry and neurophysiology.

The nature of Timpanaro's 'materialist' critique differs markedly from that of his extended, closely argued critical rebuttal of Freudian methodology. In effect, Timpanaro is offering a prescriptive account of psychology. It is not, after all, an appeal to some notion of an unconscious which separates Timpanaro from Freud and his followers. Timpanaro's own explanations presuppose the existence of unconscious mental processes: banalization, disimprovement, etc. involve a striving for mental economy, an unconscious tendency towards the exertion of least effort. All this is clearly stated by Timpanaro. What ultimately distinguishes him from other critics is his strongly held, if inadequately argued, belief that psychoanalysis is a non-materialist pseudo-science. As far as Timpanaro is concerned, the proper response to an overly rationalistic conception of the human psyche is not irrationalism – either in methodological approach or as characteristic of the 'discovered' unconscious – but a principled return to biology and neurophysiology as the foundations of a materialist psychology.

Timpanaro's arguments are, in this context, inadequate to his polemical purpose inasmuch as his synoptic criticisms of Freud have the suggestiveness, and insubstantiality, of a popular history of ideas and in so far as his point of attack presupposes the kind of materialism which he himself espouses. However, there is some merit to such an approach. In willingly embracing a 'vulgar' or 'reductionist' biological materialism, Timpanaro wilfully violates an apparently central canon of Freudian interpretation – namely, that Freud, the sophisticated psychologist of mind should, at all costs, be salvaged from the mechanistic and reductionist excesses that inform a significant part of his intellectual and scientific outlook. For Timpanaro, Freud is, on the contrary, not materialist enough. Such a critical perspective shifts the ground on which Freud is normally appreciated. We might otherwise think that the debate between Freud's defenders and detractors merely concerned the legitimacy of talking about an 'unconscious', that anti-Freudians were unrepentant subscribers to the demonstrably false Cartesian identification of psyche and consciousness. Timpanaro's virtue is to have suggested that the Freudian notion of an unconscious involves a lot more: the characterization of mental processes and the nature of a properly scientific description and explanation of these. That ultimately his work should have indicated a need without itself adequately fulfilling it is a mark of its admittedly polemical limits. However, it is a sad commentary on the way in which Freud is currently interpreted that Timpanaro's work, and its far-reaching implications, should so signally have been ignored.

Notes

1   Ludwig Wittgenstein, 'Conversations on Freud', in Richard Wollheim and James Hopkins (eds.), *Philosophical Essays on Freud* (Cambridge 1982), p. 8.
2   *The Interpretation of Dreams, SE*, IV, p. 280 and p. 311; V, p. 532.

Further reading

Foucault's views on psychoanalysis and sexuality, mentioned in all too brief passing, may be found principally in his *The History of Sexuality, Vol. 1: An Introduction* (London 1979). There is a useful critical review of this, and other thinking by Foucault on psychoanalysis, in John Forrester's, 'Michel Foucault and the History of Psychoanalysis', *History of Science*, **18** (1980), pp. 286–303.

Timpanaro's *The Freudian Slip, Psychoanalysis and Textual Criticism*, which was first published in Italy as *Il Lapsus Freudiano* (1974), appeared in an English translation by Kate Soper (London 1976). His equally stimulating *On Materialism*, many of whose arguments are relevant to his case against Freud, was also published by New Left Books in 1975.

As suggested in this chapter, the book on Freud has been received with a deafening silence. *New Left Review* chose to preview several of its chapters in its issue, no. 91. These were the subject of a set of replies by Jacqueline Rose, Juliet Mitchell and Lucien Rey, Alan Beckett and John Howe, and David Rumney (all in *New Left Review*, no. 94 (November–December 1975), pp. 74–84). A review of the complete published text, which largely shares the *NLR* reviewers' acerbically expressed contempt for Timpanaro's views, can be found in Paul Foss and Liz Gross, 'Timpanaro's Limbo', *Intervention* (Australia), no. 9 (1977), pp. 63–76. I have tried to deal with much of this criticism above. A courteous and cogently argued response by Timpanaro (*New Left Review*, no. 95 (January–February 1976)) received no further reply. *New Left Review* did publish a review of the entire book by Charles Rycroft (no. 118 (November–December 1979), pp. 81–8) who, though a Freudian, accepts the substance of Timpanaro's main criticism and concludes that there is indeed something very wrong with the concept of the 'Unconscious'.

That apart, Timpanaro's book has been the subject of no more than about two brief and unhelpful reviews. Such neglect is intellectually scandalous – particularly in view of Freud's professed importance for a significant number of British intellectuals. In the absence of any extended response, the curt and contemptuous dismissal of Timpanaro, evidenced in the *NLR*, no. 94 pieces, remains a lamentable indictment of a certain philosophical arrogance.

Conclusion

Let us start with what may now appear truistic. The senses in which the term 'unconscious' is least objectionable are those in which it is least Freudian. Many philosophers would be happy enough to speak of mental items as 'unconscious', where this means simply that they were ones of which the individual is not immediately, presently and certainly aware. There is an uninteresting use of 'unconscious' which qualifies the individual rather than the mental term: I am unaware of x, or x is something of which I am not presently aware. To the extent that I can currently and immediately be aware of, at most, a few ideas it is trivially true that there are a very large number of other ideas of which I am 'unconscious'. If, however, the term 'unconscious' qualifies the mental term, there may be the further, stronger implication that there are some mental items which I currently 'possess', but of which I am not at present aware. On one understanding of memory, for instance, I retain the experiences of past events. Though I can recall such experiences, become presently aware of the experience I had previously, these remain, for most of the time, unconscious. There may well be ways of rendering the facts of memory – in terms of a present capacity or disposition – which do not beg the question of whether there are experiences subsisting 'in', but not consciously 'present to' the mind. However, the stronger version – that there are unconscious memories – while it might not trouble philosophers, would not, of course, implicate Freud's views.

What is required for the notion of 'unconscious' to become both more interesting and more specifically Freudian are two claims: first, that the unconscious possession of a mental item is required for an adequate explanation of a current mental state or action; and, second, that there be specifiable limits to the ways in which the individual could become conscious of such an item. Now an interpretation of Freud much favoured by some Anglo-American philosophers is to see psycho-analytic explanation as analogous to ordinary explanations of present behaviour or attitudes. The only difference is that, with the former, the wants, beliefs and intentions are ones of which the agent is unaware. If, however, it is sensible to speak of unconscious wants, beliefs, etc., then these can figure in explanations of behaviour in fundamentally the same way as conscious beliefs, etc. Two things are normally claimed of this interpretation: that it captures the fullest and best sense of what Freud said, or meant to say; and that it is free, or can be freed, from philo-sophical confusion.

To take the first claim. The essence of Freud's 'discovery' lies in his having demonstrated the propriety of talking about unconscious motives, purposes, desires, etc., which differ from consciously avowed motives and purposes only in respect of their being unconscious. Freud has thereby successfully shown that large areas of human behaviour, previously dismissed as senseless and purposeless, in fact have a sense. It is, of course, necessary to show that it is coherent to speak of unconscious desires, beliefs and intentions in the required sense. Some philosophers simply deny that this is possible, and thus reject any such attempted rendering of Freud.

However, those who do favour such an account are careful to specify the sense in which the desire, belief or whatever which explains the agent's behaviour is unconscious. It has to be one the agent could and would avow as his/her own – if certain other conditions were fulfilled, if they were not so prevented by their neurotic illness. What is *meant* by an 'unconscious intention' is that it is one which the agent could avow and could be conscious of. Whether individuals *actually do* become aware of such intentions as serve to explain their behaviour is con-tingent upon the progress of the analytic cure. But, as long as Freudians understand unconscious items as those which can, in principle, become conscious, they are not guilty of incoherence. Where Freudians do err, on such an account, is in speaking of an 'unconscious mind' to which such items belong, and in employing a causal language to explain their relation to current behaviour. It is, obviously, thought unnecessary gratuitously to introduce a dubious entity, called 'the unconscious', when all that is required is the adjectival and adverbial uses of 'unconscious' to qualify the mental item employed in common-sensical explanations of behaviour. The coherent use of the adjective, 'unconscious', does not necessitate the introduction of the noun, which, in itself, raises serious and perhaps unanswerable philosophical problems.

One thing that can immediately be said about this interpretation is that it would appear not to capture the important distinction between suppression and repression. This distinction can be stated as follows. Some mental items are only temporarily excluded from, and can, with relative ease, be brought to attention; others are radically excluded from consciousness, but have a continuing effect upon behaviour. Critics, like Timpanaro for instance, might be quite prepared to concede that individuals may do or say things for reasons of which they are not at the time aware, but of which they are fairly immediately, and with comparative facility, able to become aware. The conditions which have to be fulfilled before agents can become conscious of the (suppressed) unconscious reasons for their behaviour are ones they themselves can provide. They seem to have to do, very loosely, with concentrating upon or attending to what was really in their minds when they did or said what appeared anomalous. Somewhat similarly, though obviously with vastly different surrounding assumptions, Sartre seems happy to regard 'bad faith' as dissolving under the reflective look of consciousness. None of this can be said to be the case with repression. The relevant conditions which have to be fulfilled before individuals could be conscious of the (repressed) unconscious reason for their action are more difficult clearly to specify. In a sense there is circularity in any such specification. If individuals were not so prevented by their neuroses, they could avow the unconscious reasons for their behaviour. But then the behaviour is the neurotic behaviour it is precisely because the unconscious reasons cannot be avowed.

At the successful completion of analysis, the patient can crudely be supposed to say something like: 'I see now that all along I unconsciously hated my father, and that it was this unconscious hatred which explained my obsessional need repeatedly to steal.' It was in this sense that the student's subsequent confession of his worry concerning the mistress's missed period 'confirmed' the Freudian explanation of the initial slip – the omission of 'aliquis'. However, Timpanaro argued that there are few, if any, grounds for believing that the worry in question was the unconscious reason for the slip; and that the student's eventual avowal could not be taken either to confirm or disconfirm the explanation proffered by Freud. In the above statement, the sense of 'I see now' can be given as either 'I see now that the only possible explanation for what I have been doing is . . ., though I, of course, do not have now, and have never been aware of, any such feelings', or 'I see now that I have hated my father, and, whereas previously I could only steal to express this hatred, I can now face up to these feelings which I have always had and which I have now become aware of.' The first rendering corresponds to a third-person ascription of an unconscious reason; the second to a first-person avowal. Freud himself tried to make such a distinction between a patient's merely 'intellectual' acceptance of an analytic interpretation, and the 'working-through' to a 'conviction based on lived experience'. Of course, the patient's acceptance of the interpretation no more confirms its truth than does that of a disinterested observer acquainted with all the relevant facts. The force of the second 'conviction' depends crucially on what sense, if any, can be given to 'knowing that one has had these feelings all along, albeit unconsciously'.

It is true, anyway, that if the validity of Freudian interpretation rested exclusively on such avowals there would be a dramatically reduced weight of evidence in its favour. Freudians believe, after all, that there are extremely good reasons for postulating the existence of an unconscious intention where this cannot, and even to the extent that it cannot, be avowed. These good reasons are given by additional theses concerning the formations of the unconscious, that is, the purported relations between the unconscious mental item and the conscious behaviour. No Freudian asks us completely to ignore or discount the means whereby someone comes to admit an unconscious desire, and simply accept that, since such an unconscious desire is belatedly recognized, unconscious desires do exist. What is important is that confirmation of – or at least very good grounds for – the existence of unconscious items can be given independently of any first-person avowal of them.

There is then some understandable reason for talk of 'the unconscious', in so far as we might wish to speak of a set of unconscious desires, intentions, etc. posited as existing and determining behaviour, whatever the individual might or could admit to. But there is a further and more important reason for speaking of 'the unconscious'. The view that psychoanalytic explanations are analogous to ordinary explanations presupposes that it is appropriate to talk of unconscious desires, beliefs and intentions which are just like their conscious analogues, except for the fact that the individual is not immediately aware of them. However, the import of Chapter 1 was that the real distinction to be found in Freud was not between conscious and unconscious forms of the same basic mental events, but rather between two fundamentally different kinds of mental activity.

We can repeat this claim by offering a much simplified, but *prima facie* conceivable, instance of an unconscious item which determines conscious behaviour and which is not properly Freudian. A person may currently have an attitude towards certain events or objects that results from a past experience which s/he is unable to remember, and which could thus be called 'unconscious'. Let us suppose that such a person dislikes floral wallpaper because one furnished the room where s/he was forced to spend an uncomfortable time during a protracted childhood illness. The memory of the wallpaper has simply been forgotten, not repressed. Another person might be able to admit, 'I'm afraid I cannot stand floral wallpapers; they are forever associated in my mind with the time when, as a child . . .'. The first person differs from the second only in that the connection between childhood experience and current attitude is hidden, because the experience cannot be recalled. Yet such a case seems to differ from a Freudian example in a number of ways. Clearly the infantile experience is not necessarily sexual; it is of the kind that it is possible to have consciously; and the relationship between it and the conscious behaviour is relatively straightforward. The originality of Freud's theory is that the unconscious proper has a form of mentality which differs markedly from that of consciousness and to which unconscious items are subject; and that the relations of such items to conscious behaviour is thereby considerably less than straightforward.

The problem is simply whether, if Freud's unconscious can be understood only in terms of the primary process, we can make any sense of the notion. We meet again the objection that no consistent and coherent explanation can be given of the way in which it is purported to operate. In particular, there seem to be two interrelated sets of contradictorily ascribed characteristics. On the one hand, the unconscious is an intentional psychic agent, yet possessed of a purely mechanical purposiveness; on the other hand, the unconscious is cognitively primitive, alogical, consisting of mobile and unthinking wishes, but makes a very sophisticated use of language. Unconscious primary processes are conceived of as governed by the pleasure principle. There is an uninhibited flow of wishful impulses, psychic energy, from idea to idea subject only to the avoidance of unpleasure and the procuring of pleasure. Now, we need not speak of unconscious 'intentions' or 'beliefs', only of purposive, that is goal-directed, activity. A purposeful response by the mental apparatus under the governance of the pleasure principle is clearly not the same as an intentional action done for a formulated reason.

Freud's explanatory language here is heavily influenced by the model of hydraulics: energy flows between and fills up, occupies ideas (*cathexis*), seeking an acceptable and tolerable level throughout the mental apparatus energy can be held back, dammed up or released along certain pathways. The obvious and pressing problem with this model is that it seems totally inadequate for capturing the cognitive activity of the unconscious. It is insufficient simply to speak of a mechanical, automatic movement of energy in certain directions. Let us take the crudest of examples and regard the *Jüngen/Juden* case, cited in Chapter 5, as an instance of displaced energy. We might, just, grant that the free and unbound energy of the unconscious system could flow easily from one word (*Jüngen*) to another (*Juden*), though we would find it hard to understand how their phonetic proximity did exactly facilitate such a displacement (why and how do similar sounding words become, for the purposes of flowing energy, proximate?). But, even then, we would be dealing solely with words as sound-images. We saw that Lacanianism is quite content to talk about signifiers and their inter-relationships apart from signifieds. We indicated the kinds of problem that this approach led to. But, even in our small example, it is clear that meanings are implicated. The unconscious wish concerns the speaking of the word, *Juden*, where this *means* 'Jews', where this is *understood* as a correct description of oneself and one's children, something of which one is embarrassed, etc., and this wish is understood to conflict with the conscious desire to say '*Jüngen*', meaning 'youngsters', understood as true of one's children, etc. We need only reflect on the additional complications evidenced in the 'aliquis' and 'Signorelli' examples to see the scale of the problem. For some writers this central point is sufficiently well-made simply by arguing that any wishing or desire must, of necessity, be concept-mediated, that is, involve a conception of those objects desired.

It just seems unrealistic to preserve the purely mechanistic account of flowing energy and, at the same time, to describe this unbound energy as being involved in cognitive activity, sometimes of a sophisticated conceptual or linguistic nature. Of course, for many this is taken to follow from the incompatibility of causal and intentional accounts of mental activity; for many, too, this is taken equally to follow from attempting to provide a reductionist, that is neurophysiological, explanation of what is properly psychical or mental. I have stressed the relation between these two charges at numerous points: the causal account looks plausible as, and in so far as it is, a neurophysiological account; conversely, the intentional language seems appropriate only to an explanation of the irreducibly mental or psychical. What needs immediately to be said is this: first, the purported inadequacy of Freud's neurophysiological theories should not, and cannot reasonably, be taken to demonstrate the failure of any reductionist account as such; second, opting for a dualist reading of Freud presents problems in terms of its dualism and as an interpretation of Freud.

What embarrasses critics of Freud is, perhaps understandably, the 'crudeness' of his mechanistic neurophysiology. He was, we are nevertheless reminded, the victim of his nineteenth-century scientific milieu. Ironically, some recent work has attempted to reinstate the credibility of Freud's neurophysiological researches and adapt them to a sophisticated monist theory of mind. However, it need only be said here that the contentious issue of whether a satisfactory and coherent monist explanation of cognitive activity and experience can be provided is not peculiar to discussions of 'the unconscious'. If such an account can be provided for what we would term 'consciousness', then, with some important qualifications, it might conceivably be extended to Freud's notion of 'the unconscious'.

The consequences of accepting dualism are, anyway, serious, and they have particular relevance to an understanding of Freud. His theory has a somatic, or biological, basis: the instincts. It is they which, when translated into psychical forces, provide the mental apparatus with its internal dynamism and lend psychoanalysis its biological credibility. Now, if dualism is embraced, some account is desperately required of how this 'basis' is related to, or 'translated into', the structures and operations of the psychic. A telling instance of the obfuscations produced by a failure clearly to answer such questions is provided in Laplanche's and Pontalis's *The Language of Psycho-Analysis*. What we find there is a 'language' which conceals a problem on the pretence of explicating its solution: sexual instincts lie on the 'borderline' between the somatic and the psychical; the relationship between these two is given by that of an instinct to its 'representative'; a physiological mechanism is a 'possible parallel' to a psychical one; psychical concepts like 'energy', 'cathexis' should be taken 'metaphorically', as expressing an 'analogy' between psychical operations and the workings of the nervous system.

Freud's theory of the unconscious cannot neatly be extracted from its neurophysiological and biological context. Freud thought of human beings as driven to behave in certain, rigidly determined, ways because he believed them to have a biological nature: somatic instincts which are translated into unconscious or conscious desires and thoughts. Of course, there are serious problems in understanding the nature of this 'translation'. But, to abandon physiology for purely psychical explanations is doubly mistaken. It deprives Freudianism of its material basis and fails to solve, by choosing simply to ignore, the important problems in understanding Freud. Indeed, such an approach can only multiply the problems. To speak, as Laplanche, Pontalis and others do, of 'representation', 'analogy', 'possible parallel' and 'borderline' is philosophically discreditable and probably, in the last analysis, incoherent.

It should be added that the use of an exclusively mental language yields one further dangerous temptation: the attribution of personhood to psychic agencies. Much has been made by some critics of the fact that Freud's only serious engagement with philosophy was his attendance of Franz Brentano's lectures. It is argued that Freud followed Brentano in accepting intentionality as the defining mark of consciousness, or mentality. And, it is suggested, in so far as Freud believed unconscious mental activity to be more than merely purposive and to be in fact intentional, he conceived of the unconscious as a 'conciousness'. There is little doubt that Freud, in many of his metaphorical illustrations, depicts 'the unconscious' as if it were a self-conscious agent, forming resolutions, entertaining beliefs and desires, and striving to secure its ends. Clearly the most objectionable characterization of the unconscious is in these terms – as a 'second mind', an irrational homunculus. There is no doubt too that Sartre reads Freud as if the latter were describing the human mind in terms of multiple personalities. His major criticism revolves around the issue of what kind of person/self-consciousness the censor must be in order to discharge its role. In general terms, the difficulties of making sense of the interrelationship between consciousness and the unconscious are hopelessly exacerbated once these latter are understood as distinct and separate 'personalities' equipped with self-consciousnesses.

131

Thus far all the problems concerning the Freudian notion of the unconscious have been in terms of the philosophy of mind. One last set of problems should briefly be indicated. These concern the theory of language and meaning which is implied by, or required of, Freud's theory. Clearly Lacan makes these problems most explicit and the difficulties inherent in his approach have already extensively been treated. Let us note only that we should be concerned about the plausibility of certain kinds of 'symbolic translation' by which unconscious desires result in forms of conscious action or speech. Some of the translations are straightforward and readily comprehensible expressions of the desire in question. Indeed, Freud is popularly held responsible, by virtue of his theory of symbolism, for making people more aware of, and consequently deeply embarrassed by, the extent to which they live out unutterable desires through symbolic actions. The very ease with which we tend to assume that many of our actions or words have such an ulterior meaning is the result of our having accepted, and been discomfited by, a popular Freudianism. (It took Freud himself to remind us that, sometimes, a cigar just is a cigar.)

The problems start once the nature of the translation makes unreasonable demands, not so much of the unconscious itself, but of language and meaning. We must distinguish two points. It may well be unrealistic to view the unconscious as a linguistically sophisticated, polyglot, culturally educated and super-intelligent agent. And to that extent, as in Timpanaro, unreasonable and unnecessary to accept that such an unconscious does exist. But it may not be incoherent. What *is* impossible is to require of language that, for instance, words or signifiers are entirely separate from their meanings or signifieds; that meaning is to be found in the interrelationship of words *qua* words. If indeed psychoanalysis does require such a psychoanalytic theory of language and meaning, then arguably psychoanalysis is incoherent at a level other than that of its theory of mind. As suggested earlier, that may well be the wholly unintended merit of Lacan's approach.

The problems of Freud's notion of the unconscious are not to be found at a single level. There are a number of interrelated questions: energetics and hermeneutics, intentionality and causality, neurophysiology and psychology, language and meaning. No single account, either sympathetic or critical, has been shown successfully and adequately to render Freud in a way that does full justice to all these different problems. It may indeed be the case that no account can satisfactorily resolve all these problems. It will then have to be admitted that, concerning 'the unconscious', Freud has not clearly shown anything.

Index